EPA 608
STUDY GUIDE

The most comprehensive test prep with realistic exam simulations and a full study plan. Includes 1000+ practice questions and detailed explanations. Boost your HVACR career!

© Copyright 2024 by Jeremy Crainstone - All rights reserved

The content within this book may not be reproduced, duplicated, or transmitted without direct written permission from the author or the publisher. Under no circumstances will any blame or legal responsibility be held against the publisher, or author, for any damages, reparation, or monetary loss due to the information contained within this book. Either directly or indirectly.

Legal Notice:

This book is copyright protected. This book is only for personal use. You cannot amend, distribute, sell, use, quote or paraphrase any part, or the content within this book, without the consent of the author or publisher.

Disclaimer Notice:

Please note the information contained within this document is for educational and entertainment purposes only. All effort has been executed to present accurate, up to date, and reliable, complete information. No warranties of any kind are declared or implied. Readers acknowledge that the author is not engaging in the rendering of legal, financial, medical, or professional advice. The content within this book has been derived from various sources. Please consult a licensed professional before attempting any techniques outlined in this book. By reading this document, the reader agrees that under no circumstances is the author responsible for any losses, direct or indirect, which are incurred as a result of the use of the information contained within this document, including, but not limited to, errors, omissions, or inaccuracies.

TABLE OF CONTENTS

INTRODUCTION 8
    EXAM STRUCTURE OVERVIEW 8
    EPA 608 CERTIFICATION IMPORTANCE 8

CHAPTER 1: CORE 10
    ENVIRONMENTAL IMPACTS 10
        Ozone Destruction by Chlorine 10
        Chlorine in CFC and HCFC Refrigerants 11
        CFC, HCFC, and HFC Refrigerant Types 13
        CFCs, HCFCs, and HFCs: Ozone Depletion Potential 14
        Atmospheric Effects of Refrigerants 15
        Stratospheric Ozone Depletion Effects 16
        Stratospheric Ozone Depletion and CFCs 18
    CLEAN AIR ACT & MONTREAL PROTOCOL 19
        CFC Phaseout Date 19
        R-22 Phaseout Date 20
        Venting Prohibition During Servicing 20
        Venting Prohibition at Disposal 21
        Prohibition on Venting Refrigerants 22
        Maximum Penalty Under Clean Air Act 23
        Montreal Protocol 23
    SECTION 608 REGULATIONS 25
        High and Low-Pressure Refrigerants 25
        System-Dependent vs. Self-Contained Equipment 26
        Equipment Covered by the Rule 27
        Third-Party Certification for Recycling 28
        Reclaimed Refrigerant Standard 29
        The Sales Restriction 30
        Clean Air Act Venting Prohibition 31
    SUBSTITUTE REFRIGERANTS AND OILS 32
        Absence of Refrigerants 32

- *Refrigerant and Lubricant Incompatibility* 33
- *Fractionation and Component Leakage* 34

REFRIGERATION 35
- *Refrigerant States and Pressures* 35
- *Refrigeration Gauges Usage and Codes* 36
- *Leak Detection* 36

THREE R DEFINITIONS 38
- *Recover* 38
- *Recycle* 39
- *Reclaim* 40

RECOVERY TECHNIQUES 41
- *Avoid Mixing Refrigerants* 41
- *Factors Affecting Recovery Speed* 42

DEHYDRATION EVACUATION 42
- *Evacuating Systems for Air and Moisture Removal* 42

SAFETY 43
- *Refrigerant Exposure Risks* 43
- *Personal Protective Equipment* 44
- *Reusable Refrigerants* 44
- *Risks of Overfilling Cylinders* 45
- *Nitrogen for Leak Detection* 45

SHIPPING 46
- *Refrigerant Cylinder Labeling Requirements* 46

CHAPTER 2: TYPE 1 SMALL APPLIANCES 47

RECOVERY REQUIREMENTS 47
- *Definition* 47
- *Evacuation for Small Appliances Pre-1993* 47
- *Evacuation for Small Appliances* 48

RECOVERY TECHNIQUES 49
- *Identifying Refrigerants and Noncondensables* 49
- *Recovering Refrigerant from Small Appliances* 51
- *Installing Access Valves for Refrigerant Recovery* 52
- *Operating Compressors for Refrigerant Recovery* 53
- *Removing Solderless Access Fittings* 54
- *HFC-134a as Substitute for CFC-12* 55

SAFETY 55
 Refrigerant Decomposition at High Temps 55

CHAPTER 3: TYPE 2 (HIGH-PRESSURE) 57

LEAK DETECTION 57
 Leakage Signs in High-Pressure Systems 57
 Leak Testing Before Charging Equipment 58
 Leak Test Gas Preference Order 59

LEAK REPAIR REQUIREMENTS 60
 Allowable Leak Rate for Refrigeration 60
 Allowable Leak Rate for Large Appliances 61
 Leak Repair Recordkeeping 62

RECOVERY TECHNIQUES 63
 Speeding Up Recovery Process 63
 Speeding Recovery Methods 64
 Reducing Contamination with New Refrigerants 65
 Checking System Pressure Stability 66

RECOVERY REQUIREMENTS 67
 Evacuation for High-Pressure Appliance Disposal 67
 Evacuation for Major vs. Non-Major Repairs 68
 Evacuation for Leaky vs. Non-Leaky Appliances 71
 Evacuation for High-Pressure Appliances 72
 Evacuation for Pre/Post-1993 Equipment 74
 Prohibition on System-Dependent Equipment 75

REFRIGERATION 76
 Identifying Refrigerants in Appliances 76
 Pressure-Temperature of High-Pressure Refrigerants 78
 High-Pressure Appliance Components 79

SAFETY 80
 Energizing Compressors Under Vacuum 80
 ASHRAE Standard 15 Equipment Room Requirements 81

CHAPTER 3: TYPE 3 LOW-PRESSURE SYSTEMS 82

LEAK DETECTION 82
 Leak Test Pressurization Methods 82
 Signs of Leakage in Low-Pressure Systems 82

Maximum Leak Test Pressure 83

Leak Inspection for High Leak Rate 84

LEAK REPAIR REQUIREMENTS 85

Annual Leak Rate for Refrigeration 85

Annual Leak Rate for Large Appliances 86

RECOVERY TECHNIQUES 87

Speeding Up Liquid Recovery Process 87

Recovering Vapor and Liquid 88

Heating Oil to 130°F for Safety 89

Prevent Freezing During Refrigerant Evacuation 90

High-Pressure Cut-Out in Recovery Devices 92

RECHARGING TECHNIQUES 93

Prevent Freezing: Vapor Before Liquid 93

Charging Centrifugals via Evaporator Valve 94

RECOVERY REQUIREMENTS 95

Evacuation for Low-Pressure Disposal 95

Evacuation for Low-Pressure Repairs 96

Evacuation for Leaky vs. Non-Leaky Appliances 97

Evacuation for Low-Pressure Appliances 99

Evacuation for Pre/Post-1993 Equipment 100

Pressurizing Low-Pressure Systems 101

Recovery Vacuum Pressure Check 102

REFRIGERATION 103

Purge Unit in Low-Pressure Systems 103

Pressure-Temperature in Low-Pressure Refrigerants 104

SAFETY 105

ASHRAE 15 Equipment Room Requirements 105

ASHRAE 15: R-123 Refrigerant Sensor 106

CONCLUSION **107**

HOW TO DOWNLOAD YOUR BONUSES

With the purchase of this book, you gain free access to numerous online resources such as in-depth videos and quiz simulations on our web app. To fully prepare for the exam, the book alone is not enough; therefore, I strongly recommend that you also review all the free resources that complement your preparation for the EPA 608 Certification. Both the videos and the other free resources allow you to dive deeper into all the topics covered in the test.

I chose not to include charts or tables in the book because I preferred to provide you with in-depth videos explaining each table and chart you need to know. Scan the QR code to access all the free resources!

SCAN THIS QR CODE:

Introduction

Exam Structure Overview

The EPA 608 Exam is structured to assess the knowledge and skills necessary for handling refrigerants within four main sections: Core, Type 1, Type 2, and Type 3 certifications. Each section targets specific competencies related to environmental safety and the proper management of refrigerants. The Core section is mandatory for all candidates, covering topics such as ozone depletion, global warming potential, and the Clean Air Act. It lays the foundational knowledge required for understanding the environmental impact of refrigerants and the regulations governing their use.

Type 1 certification focuses on small appliances, requiring knowledge of recovery techniques, safety standards, and the identification of different refrigerants. This section is crucial for technicians working with devices like domestic refrigerators, window air conditioners, and vending machines.

Type 2 certification delves into high-pressure refrigerants, emphasizing leak detection, repair practices, and recovery requirements for equipment such as residential air conditioners and heat pumps. It is designed for technicians servicing or disposing of appliances with a high potential for ozone depletion or global warming.

Type 3 certification covers low-pressure refrigerants, with a focus on large, commercial systems like chillers. It tests the ability to manage refrigerants in a way that minimizes environmental impact, including proper recovery, evacuation, and recharging techniques.

Each section consists of multiple-choice questions, designed to test practical knowledge and understanding of regulations. The exam requires thorough preparation, as it covers a wide range of topics from scientific principles to specific regulatory details. Success on the EPA 608 Exam opens up significant professional opportunities, ensuring compliance with environmental laws and contributing to the protection of the planet.

EPA 608 Certification Importance

The EPA 608 Certification is a critical credential for HVACR technicians, signifying their proficiency in handling refrigerants in a manner that protects the environment and complies with federal regulations. Achieving this certification is not merely a professional milestone; it is a legal requirement for anyone who seeks to work with refrigeration and air-conditioning systems, particularly those that involve controlled substances known to deplete the ozone layer or contribute to global warming. The certification encompasses a broad range of knowledge, from understanding the environmental impact of refrigerants to mastering the technical skills required for their proper recovery, recycling, and disposal.

Holding an EPA 608 Certification demonstrates a technician's commitment to environmental stewardship, a quality increasingly valued in today's eco-conscious market. It opens doors to job opportunities that are otherwise inaccessible to uncertified individuals, offering a competitive edge in the HVACR industry. This certification is not just about fulfilling a regulatory requirement; it's about equipping technicians with the knowledge and skills to make environmentally responsible decisions in their daily work. It underscores the importance of minimizing the release of harmful refrigerants into the atmosphere, thereby contributing to the global effort to repair the ozone layer and reduce greenhouse gas emissions.

For businesses, employing EPA 608 certified technicians is a testament to their dedication to environmental protection and regulatory compliance, enhancing their reputation and trustworthiness in the eyes of customers and partners. It also mitigates the risk of legal and financial penalties that can arise from non-compliance with environmental laws.

In essence, the EPA 608 Certification is indispensable for anyone involved in the HVACR sector, serving as a foundation for a sustainable and responsible career in an industry at the forefront of combating climate change. It is a tangible reflection of a technician's expertise, professionalism, and commitment to preserving the planet for future generations.

Chapter 1: Core

Environmental Impacts

Ozone Destruction by Chlorine

The destruction of ozone by chlorine is a critical environmental issue that directly impacts the Earth's stratospheric ozone layer, the protective shield that absorbs the sun's harmful ultraviolet radiation. Chlorine atoms, originating from chlorofluorocarbons (CFCs) and hydrochlorofluorocarbons (HCFCs), play a significant role in ozone depletion. When CFCs and HCFCs are released into the atmosphere, they are eventually broken down by ultraviolet radiation, releasing chlorine atoms. A single chlorine atom can destroy thousands of ozone molecules before it is removed from the stratosphere, leading to the thinning of the ozone layer, particularly evident in the phenomenon known as the ozone hole over Antarctica. The mechanism by which chlorine destroys ozone is a catalytic cycle. In this process, a chlorine atom reacts with an ozone (O_3) molecule, resulting in the formation of chlorine monoxide (ClO) and a molecule of oxygen (O_2). Subsequently, the chlorine monoxide reacts with a free oxygen atom, regenerating the chlorine atom and producing another molecule of oxygen. This regenerated chlorine atom is then free to repeat the cycle, destroying more ozone molecules. The efficiency of this cycle is such that it significantly contributes to the depletion of the stratospheric ozone layer, which is crucial for life on Earth as it protects living organisms from excessive ultraviolet radiation.

The environmental implications of ozone depletion are profound. Increased levels of ultraviolet radiation reaching the Earth's surface can lead to higher incidences of skin cancer, cataracts, and other health issues in humans. It can also affect ecosystems, particularly those in aquatic environments, and can harm agricultural productivity by damaging sensitive crops. Recognizing the global scale of this issue, the international community adopted the Montreal Protocol on Substances that Deplete the Ozone Layer, aiming to phase out the production and consumption of ozone-depleting substances, including CFCs and HCFCs. This landmark agreement has led to a decrease in the atmospheric concentration of these compounds, offering hope for the gradual recovery of the ozone layer.

However, the persistence of CFCs and HCFCs in the atmosphere due to their long atmospheric lifetimes means that the issue of ozone depletion will continue to be a concern for the foreseeable future. The role of chlorine in this process underscores the importance of strict regulatory measures and the need for continued vigilance in monitoring atmospheric concentrations of ozone-depleting substances. As HVACR technicians and professionals, understanding the impact of refrigerants on the ozone layer is crucial. This knowledge not only informs best practices in refrigerant management but also highlights the importance of transitioning to refrigerants with lower ozone depletion potential. The critical role of HVACR professionals in mitigating the impact of chlorine-based refrigerants on ozone depletion cannot be overstated. With the phasedown of CFCs and HCFCs under the Montreal Protocol, the industry has seen a shift towards the use of hydrofluorocarbons (HFCs) and, more recently, hydrofluoroolefins (HFOs) and natural refrigerants, which have no ozone depletion potential (ODP) and lower global warming potential (GWP). This transition is pivotal in the global effort to protect the stratospheric ozone layer and reduce the impact of climate change.

Technicians must be adept at handling, recovering, and properly disposing of old refrigerants, ensuring that these substances do not escape into the atmosphere. The adoption of best practices in refrigerant management, including the use of advanced recovery and recycling equipment, is essential in minimizing the release of ozone-depleting substances. Furthermore, staying informed about the latest developments in refrigerant technology and regulations is crucial for professionals in the field. This includes understanding the implications of the Kigali Amendment to the Montreal Protocol, which aims to phase down the production and consumption of HFCs globally. The responsibility also extends to educating customers and the community about the importance of selecting and maintaining HVACR systems that use environmentally friendly refrigerants. By promoting the use of systems with lower ODP and GWP, HVACR professionals play a direct role in reducing the environmental impact of cooling and refrigeration systems. In addition to regulatory compliance, the shift towards sustainable refrigeration practices offers economic benefits. Systems designed to use less harmful refrigerants are often more energy-efficient, leading to lower operational costs over time. This aligns with the growing demand for green building practices and can enhance the marketability of HVACR services.

The journey towards a fully sustainable HVACR industry is ongoing, and the role of each technician is critical in this global effort. By embracing new technologies, adhering to best practices in refrigerant management, and advocating for environmentally responsible choices, HVACR professionals can significantly contribute to the healing of the ozone layer and the protection of the planet. This commitment to environmental stewardship not only addresses the immediate challenges of ozone depletion but also contributes to the broader goal of mitigating climate change, ensuring a healthier environment for future generations.

Chlorine in CFC and HCFC Refrigerants

Chlorofluorocarbons (CFCs) and hydrochlorofluorocarbons (HCFCs) have been integral to various industries, notably in refrigeration and air conditioning systems, due to their stability, non-flammability, and efficiency in heat absorption. However, the presence of chlorine in these compounds has significant environmental repercussions, particularly concerning the depletion of the stratospheric ozone layer. When CFCs and HCFCs are released into the atmosphere, either through leaks, improper handling, or disposal, they ascend to the stratosphere. Here, ultraviolet

(UV) radiation breaks these molecules down, releasing chlorine atoms. The chlorine acts as a catalyst in the destruction of ozone molecules, a process that significantly thins the protective ozone layer and increases the amount of harmful UV radiation reaching the Earth's surface. The chemistry behind the ozone depletion process is both fascinating and alarming. A single chlorine atom can destroy over 100,000 ozone molecules before it is neutralized or exits the stratosphere. This destructive capability underscores the urgency in managing these substances with utmost care. The role of chlorine from CFCs and HCFCs in ozone depletion is not merely a chemical curiosity; it represents a critical challenge for environmental policy and the HVACR industry's practices. Given the global recognition of the threat posed by ozone depletion, international agreements such as the Montreal Protocol have mandated the phase-out of CFCs and HCFCs, pushing for a transition to less harmful substances. The HVACR industry has been at the forefront of adapting to these changes, seeking alternatives that do not contribute to ozone layer depletion while maintaining the efficiency and safety standards required for cooling and refrigeration applications.

The transition away from CFCs and HCFCs involves not only the adoption of new, more environmentally friendly refrigerants but also significant changes in equipment design, maintenance practices, and technician training. Understanding the properties of alternative refrigerants, including their environmental impacts, compatibility with existing systems, and handling requirements, is crucial for technicians. This knowledge ensures that the industry can move forward in a manner that protects the environment while continuing to meet the cooling needs of society. The presence of chlorine in CFCs and HCFCs and its environmental impact is a complex issue that intertwines chemistry, environmental science, policy, and industry practices. As we delve deeper into the specifics of how chlorine contributes to ozone depletion and explore the efforts to mitigate this impact, it becomes clear that the role of HVACR professionals is not just about maintaining comfortable indoor temperatures. It's about contributing to a larger global effort to protect the stratospheric ozone layer, a critical component of Earth's life-support system. This responsibility entails staying informed about the latest developments in refrigerant technology, adhering to best practices in refrigerant management, and actively participating in the industry's transition towards more sustainable practices.

The imperative for HVACR technicians to engage in environmentally responsible refrigerant management extends beyond regulatory compliance. It encompasses a commitment to safeguarding our planet's atmospheric health. The intricate relationship between chlorine-based refrigerants and ozone depletion necessitates a proactive approach to refrigerant handling. This includes meticulous leak detection, rigorous maintenance protocols, and the adoption of recovery and recycling technologies that prevent the release of these substances into the atmosphere. The environmental stewardship role of HVACR professionals is pivotal in ensuring that the transition away from CFCs and HCFCs is executed effectively, minimizing the environmental footprint of refrigeration and air conditioning systems.

As the industry evolves, the introduction of alternative refrigerants with lower ozone depletion potential (ODP) and global warming potential (GWP) marks a significant advancement in environmental protection efforts. However, the transition is not without challenges. The compatibility of new refrigerants with existing systems, the need for updated safety protocols due to different chemical properties, and the economic implications of retrofitting or replacing equipment are all critical considerations. These factors underscore the importance of comprehensive training and education programs for technicians, equipping them with the knowledge and skills necessary to navigate the complexities of modern refrigerant management. Moreover, the role of HVACR professionals in educating consumers and businesses about the benefits of adopting systems that utilize environmentally friendly refrigerants cannot be underestimated. By advocating for energy-efficient, low-impact refrigeration and air conditioning solutions, technicians can influence market trends and consumer preferences, further driving the industry towards sustainability.

CFC, HCFC, and HFC Refrigerant Types

Understanding the distinct characteristics and environmental impacts of **CFCs (Chlorofluorocarbons)**, **HCFCs (Hydrochlorofluorocarbons)**, and **HFCs (Hydrofluorocarbo)** is crucial for HVACR professionals aiming to make informed decisions regarding refrigerant use and management. CFCs, such as **R-12**, have been largely phased out due to their high **Ozone Depletion Potential (ODP)** and significant global warming potential. These substances were once common in refrigeration, air conditioning, and aerosol propellants but are now recognized for their detrimental effects on the stratospheric ozone layer.

HCFCs, including **R-22**, were introduced as transitional substitutes for CFCs, offering lower ODP while still contributing to global warming. Although HCFCs are less harmful than CFCs, they are also subject to phase-out schedules under international agreements like the **Montreal Protocol** due to their lingering environmental impacts. The shift from CFCs to HCFCs marked a significant step in reducing harm to the ozone layer, yet it was clear that further changes were necessary to address climate change concerns. The introduction of HFCs, such as **R-134a**, represented a move towards refrigerants with no ODP. HFCs do not contain chlorine, which is responsible for ozone depletion. However, many HFCs have high **Global Warming Potential (GWP)**, leading to their scrutiny under climate change regulations. The evolution from CFCs to HCFCs, and eventually to HFCs, reflects the HVACR industry's ongoing efforts to balance operational needs with environmental responsibility.

The transition to **low-GWP refrigerants** is the industry's current focus, with newer substances like **HFOs (Hydrofluoroolefins)** and natural refrigerants gaining popularity due to their minimal environmental impact. This shift underscores the importance of staying informed about refrigerant regulations, understanding the characteristics of various refrigerants, and adopting best practices for their use and disposal. For HVACR professionals, recognizing the type of refrigerant in use—whether it's a CFC, HCFC, or HFC—is not just about compliance with regulations; it's about contributing to a larger effort to protect the environment while ensuring the safety and efficiency of refrigeration and air conditioning systems. As the industry moves forward, the knowledge of these substances and the implications of their use will remain a cornerstone of responsible HVACR practice, highlighting the need for continuous education and adaptation to emerging technologies and environmental standards.

CFCs, HCFCs, and HFCs: Ozone Depletion Potential

Understanding the hierarchy of ozone-depletion potential (ODP) among **CFCs**, **HCFCs**, and **HFCs** is pivotal for HVACR professionals who are committed to environmental stewardship. This knowledge not only aids in compliance with regulations but also in making informed decisions that minimize environmental impact. **Chlorofluorocarbons (CFCs)**, once prevalent in the industry due to their stability and efficiency as refrigerants, have been identified as the most detrimental to the ozone layer. Their molecules contain chlorine, which, upon release into the atmosphere and subsequent exposure to ultraviolet radiation, breaks down and releases chlorine atoms. These chlorine atoms act as catalysts in the chemical breakdown of ozone molecules, a process that can be repeated thousands of times by a single chlorine atom, thus significantly depleting the stratospheric ozone layer. Transitioning to **Hydrochlorofluorocarbons (HCFCs)** was an interim solution aimed at reducing the adverse environmental impacts associated with CFCs. HCFCs, while still containing chlorine and thus capable of depleting the ozone layer, have a lower ODP due to their ability to break down more readily in the lower atmosphere, preventing a significant portion of chlorine from reaching the stratosphere. This characteristic, combined with a phasedown schedule under international treaties, marked a critical step towards mitigating ozone depletion. However, the presence of chlorine in HCFCs still poses a risk to the ozone layer, necessitating further evolution towards more environmentally friendly refrigerants.

Hydrofluorocarbons (HFCs) emerged as the next generation of refrigerants, designed to eliminate the ozone depletion issue associated with chlorine. HFCs do not contain chlorine, thereby having an ODP of zero. This significant advantage positions HFCs as a preferable choice in applications where minimizing environmental impact is a priority. However, it's crucial to note that while HFCs solve the problem of ozone depletion, many possess high global warming potentials (GWP), shifting the environmental focus towards finding solutions that address both ozone and climate impacts. The ongoing development and adoption of refrigerants with low environmental impact, such as **Hydrofluoroolefins (HFOs)** and natural refrigerants, reflect the HVACR industry's commitment to innovation and environmental responsibility. These advancements underscore the importance of continuous learning and adaptation by HVACR professionals to stay abreast of emerging technologies and refrigerants that offer both operational efficiency and environmental sustainability.

Atmospheric Effects of Refrigerants

The atmospheric effects of refrigerants extend beyond the immediate vicinity of their release, influencing global climate patterns and the integrity of the ozone layer. The release of CFCs, HCFCs, and HFCs into the atmosphere has been a significant concern due to their contribution to ozone depletion and global warming. The ozone layer, a critical shield protecting the Earth from harmful ultraviolet (UV) radiation, has been compromised by the release of chlorine and bromine atoms found in these refrigerants. The breakdown of ozone molecules leads to an increase in UV radiation reaching the Earth's surface, which can result in higher rates of skin cancer, cataracts, and other health issues in humans, as well as detrimental effects on wildlife and marine ecosystems.

Global warming, another significant atmospheric effect of refrigerants, is primarily driven by the greenhouse gas effect. Certain refrigerants, particularly those with high Global Warming Potential (GWP), trap heat in the Earth's atmosphere, leading to an increase in global temperatures. This rise in temperature contributes to climate change, manifesting in more extreme weather events, melting polar ice caps, rising sea levels, and shifts in biodiversity. HFCs, while not depleting the ozone layer, have been identified as potent greenhouse gases due to their high GWP. The environmental impact of these refrigerants has prompted the development and adoption of alternatives with lower GWP, such as Hydrofluoroolefins (HFOs) and natural refrigerants, which offer reduced global warming potential without compromising the ozone layer. The transition to these low-GWP refrigerants is critical in mitigating the atmospheric effects of traditional refrigerants. However, the process involves challenges, including compatibility with existing systems, cost implications, and the need for technician training. The HVACR industry plays a pivotal role in this transition, requiring professionals to stay informed about emerging refrigerants, understand their environmental impacts, and adopt best practices in refrigerant management. Proper recovery, recycling, and disposal of refrigerants are essential measures to prevent their release into the atmosphere, thereby minimizing their environmental footprint.

The regulatory landscape surrounding refrigerants continues to evolve, with international agreements like the Montreal Protocol and its Kigali Amendment playing a crucial role in phasing down the use of high-GWP refrigerants. Compliance with these regulations not only contributes to environmental protection but also ensures that HVACR professionals remain competitive in a market that increasingly values sustainability. In the context of atmospheric effects, the role of refrigerants is a double-edged sword, offering essential services in refrigeration and air conditioning while posing significant environmental challenges. The ongoing efforts to develop and implement environmentally friendly refrigerants are testament to the HVACR industry's commitment to sustainability and environmental stewardship. As technology advances, the selection and management of refrigerants will continue to be a key factor in addressing the dual challenges of ozone depletion and global warming, underscoring the importance of informed decision-making and responsible practices in the HVACR field.

Stratospheric Ozone Depletion Effects

The depletion of the stratospheric ozone layer presents significant health and environmental challenges that extend far beyond the immediate areas of ozone thinning. The stratospheric ozone layer acts as a protective shield for the Earth, absorbing the majority of the sun's harmful ultraviolet (UV) radiation. Without this protective layer, more intense UV radiation reaches the Earth's surface, leading to a host of adverse effects on human health, ecosystems, and the environment at large. One of the most direct impacts of increased UV exposure on humans is the heightened risk of skin cancers, including melanoma and non-melanoma types. The relationship between ozone depletion and skin cancer rates is well-documented, with studies indicating a clear increase in incidence rates in populations exposed to higher levels of UV radiation due to thinning ozone.

In addition to skin cancer, increased UV radiation can lead to serious eye conditions, such as cataracts, which is a leading cause of blindness globally. The correlation between UV exposure and the acceleration of cataract development underscores the critical role the ozone layer plays in safeguarding human health against debilitating conditions. Moreover, the immune system is not spared from the effects of increased UV radiation. There is evidence to suggest that overexposure to UV radiation can suppress the immune response, making individuals more susceptible to infections and reducing the efficacy of vaccines. This aspect of ozone depletion is particularly concerning, as it implies broader public health implications beyond the direct effects of UV exposure. The environmental consequences of stratospheric ozone depletion are equally profound. Ecosystems, particularly those in aquatic environments, are highly sensitive to changes in UV radiation levels. Phytoplankton, the foundation of aquatic food webs, exhibits decreased productivity and altered reproductive patterns under increased UV exposure, leading to cascading effects on marine biodiversity and fisheries. Such disruptions not only threaten marine life but also the livelihoods of communities dependent on these resources. Terrestrial ecosystems are not immune to the impacts of ozone depletion. Increased UV radiation affects plant growth, photosynthesis, and nutrient cycling, with potential implications for global food security and biodiversity. The intricate interplay between ozone depletion and climate change adds another layer of complexity to the environmental impacts. Certain substances that contribute to ozone layer thinning also possess potent greenhouse gas properties, further exacerbating global warming and climate change. This dual role highlights the need for integrated approaches to address both ozone depletion and climate change, recognizing the interconnectedness of these global environmental challenges. As the HVACR industry continues to evolve in response to these environmental imperatives, the role of professionals in the field becomes increasingly critical. Understanding the mechanisms of ozone depletion and its wide-ranging effects empowers HVACR technicians to make informed decisions about refrigerant management, contributing to global efforts to restore the ozone layer and mitigate climate change. The transition to refrigerants with lower ozone depletion and global warming potentials is a key aspect of this endeavor, underscoring the importance of staying abreast of regulatory developments and technological advancements in the field. The detrimental effects of stratospheric ozone depletion extend to wildlife as well, with numerous studies highlighting the vulnerability of certain species to increased UV radiation. Amphibians, for instance, have been particularly affected, experiencing higher mortality rates, developmental deformities, and decreased reproductive success. These outcomes not only signal a direct threat to biodiversity but also indicate the potential for significant shifts in ecosystem dynamics and stability. The increased UV radiation that results from ozone layer thinning can also lead to the degradation of materials, including plastics, wood, fabrics, and rubber, shortening the lifespan of products and contributing to economic losses. This aspect of ozone depletion underscores the broad spectrum of consequences that transcend environmental and health impacts, touching upon economic and societal dimensions as well.

In addressing the challenges posed by stratospheric ozone depletion, the role of policy and regulation becomes paramount. The Montreal Protocol, an international treaty designed to phase out the production and consumption of ozone-depleting substances, has played a crucial role in the efforts to protect and restore the ozone layer. The success of the Montreal Protocol demonstrates the effectiveness of global cooperation in tackling environmental issues, serving as a model for addressing other pressing challenges such as climate change. The ongoing amendments and adjustments to the protocol reflect the dynamic nature of environmental science and the need for policies to adapt to new findings and technological advancements. For HVACR professionals, the implications of stratospheric ozone depletion highlight the importance of responsible refrigerant management practices. Proper recovery, recycling, and disposal of refrigerants are essential to preventing the release of ozone-depleting substances into the atmosphere. Additionally, the adoption of alternative refrigerants with lower environmental impacts is a critical step toward minimizing the HVACR industry's contribution to ozone depletion and global warming. The commitment to environmental stewardship in the HVACR field is not only a matter of regulatory compliance but also a reflection of the industry's broader responsibility to society and the planet.

The interconnectedness of ozone depletion, climate change, and human activity underscores the complexity of the environmental challenges facing the world today. It is clear that the actions taken to protect the ozone layer have broader implications for global environmental health, emphasizing the need for an integrated approach to sustainability. As the HVACR industry continues to navigate these challenges, the knowledge and practices of its professionals will be instrumental in shaping a sustainable future. The efforts to mitigate ozone depletion and its effects are a testament to the potential for human ingenuity and cooperation to address global environmental issues, reinforcing the importance of continued vigilance, innovation, and commitment to environmental protection.

Stratospheric Ozone Depletion and CFCs

The evidence of stratospheric ozone depletion is both compelling and concerning, with Chlorofluorocarbons (CFCs) and Hydrochlorofluorocarbons (HCFCs) playing a significant role in this environmental challenge. The stratospheric ozone layer, essential for protecting the Earth from the sun's harmful ultraviolet radiation, has been under threat due to the release of these substances into the atmosphere. The mechanism by which CFCs and HCFCs contribute to ozone depletion is well understood, involving the release of chlorine and bromine atoms when these compounds are broken down by ultraviolet light. These atoms then participate in ozone-depleting reactions that can destroy ozone molecules at a much faster rate than they can be naturally created.

Scientific studies have provided clear evidence of the link between the use of CFCs and HCFCs and the thinning of the ozone layer, most notably observed as the ozone hole over Antarctica. This phenomenon was first observed in the 1980s, leading to international concern and action. The size and depth of the ozone hole have varied over the years, with temperature and atmospheric dynamics playing a role, but the underlying cause remains the presence of ozone-depleting substances. Measurements from satellites, ground stations, and balloons have shown a decrease in stratospheric ozone concentrations globally, not just over the poles, highlighting the widespread impact of these chemicals.

The implications of stratospheric ozone depletion are far-reaching, affecting not just human health but also ecosystems around the world. Increased levels of UV radiation reaching the Earth's surface can lead to higher rates of skin cancer and cataracts in humans, as well as impacting plant life and aquatic ecosystems. The recognition of these impacts led to the adoption of the Montreal Protocol in 1987, an international treaty aimed at phasing out the production and consumption of ozone-depleting substances, including CFCs and HCFCs.

The transition away from CFCs and HCFCs has involved the development and adoption of alternative refrigerants with lower ozone depletion potential. This shift has been critical in efforts to protect and restore the ozone layer, with recent reports suggesting that the ozone layer is slowly recovering. However, the persistence of CFCs and HCFCs in the atmosphere due to their long atmospheric lifetimes means that the ozone layer will take several decades to fully recover.

For HVACR professionals, understanding the environmental impact of refrigerants is crucial. The phase-out of CFCs and HCFCs represents a significant step forward in environmental protection, but it also necessitates adaptation and change within the industry. Technicians must be knowledgeable about the refrigerants they work with, not only to ensure compliance with regulations but also to contribute to broader environmental stewardship efforts. The move towards refrigerants with lower global warming potential and zero ozone depletion potential is an ongoing process, requiring continuous learning and adaptation. The evidence of stratospheric ozone depletion and the role of CFCs and HCFCs underscore the importance of responsible refrigerant management. Proper recovery, recycling, and disposal practices are essential to prevent the release of these and other harmful substances into the atmosphere. As the HVACR industry continues to evolve, the commitment to environmental protection and sustainability remains a key priority, reflecting the collective responsibility to safeguard the planet for future generations. The role of HVACR professionals in this effort is critical, highlighting the need for ongoing education, certification, and adherence to best practices in refrigerant management.

Clean Air Act & Montreal Protocol

CFC Phaseout Date

The **Clean Air Act** and the **Montreal Protocol** have set forth specific timelines for the phaseout of **Chlorofluorocarbons (CFCs)**, reflecting a global commitment to environmental protection and the restoration of the ozone layer. The pivotal date marking the beginning of the end for CFCs in the United States was January 1, 1996. From this date forward, the production and import of most CFCs were banned, underscoring a significant regulatory milestone in the fight against ozone depletion. This prohibition was a direct response to scientific evidence linking CFCs to the thinning of the stratospheric ozone layer, a condition with far-reaching implications for human health, ecosystems, and the climate.

The phaseout of CFCs did not occur in isolation but was part of a broader strategy under the **Montreal Protocol** to eliminate substances known to deplete the ozone layer. The protocol, an international treaty ratified by countries worldwide, has been instrumental in phasing out the production and consumption of ozone-depleting substances. The success of these regulatory measures is evident in the gradual recovery of the ozone layer, a testament to the effectiveness of coordinated global action in addressing environmental challenges. For HVACR professionals, the phaseout dates of CFCs and other refrigerants under the **Clean Air Act** and the **Montreal Protocol** are more than historical footnotes. They represent critical junctures in the industry's evolution towards more sustainable practices. The transition away from CFCs has necessitated the adoption of alternative refrigerants with lower ozone depletion potentials, a shift that has implications for equipment design, maintenance, and repair. Understanding these regulatory milestones is essential for compliance, but it also underscores the HVACR industry's role in environmental stewardship.

As the industry continues to adapt to these changes, HVACR professionals must remain informed about ongoing and future regulatory developments. The phaseout of CFCs is a key chapter in the broader narrative of the HVACR industry's response to environmental challenges. It highlights the importance of innovation, adaptation, and education in ensuring that the industry not only complies with regulatory mandates but also contributes positively to global environmental goals.

R-22 Phaseout Date

The phaseout of R-22, a hydrochlorofluorocarbon (HCFC) refrigerant, is a critical component of the global initiative to protect the stratospheric ozone layer. Under the Montreal Protocol, an international treaty designed to phase out the production and consumption of ozone-depleting substances (ODS), R-22 has been identified for gradual elimination. In the United States, the Environmental Protection Agency (EPA) has implemented regulations that align with the Montreal Protocol's objectives, setting specific deadlines for the phaseout of HCFCs, including R-22. The production and importation of R-22 in the U.S. were prohibited starting January 1, 2020. This regulatory action does not ban the use of R-22 in existing systems but limits the availability of this refrigerant to reclaimed and recycled quantities only. The aim is to encourage the HVAC industry to transition to alternative refrigerants with lower ozone depletion potential (ODP) and global warming potential (GWP). The phaseout schedule has been designed to allow for a gradual transition, minimizing disruption to the industry and consumers while maximizing environmental benefits. Technicians and stakeholders in the HVACR industry must be aware of the implications of the R-22 phaseout. The limited availability of R-22 and the eventual need to replace or retrofit existing equipment that uses this refrigerant underscore the importance of understanding and complying with EPA regulations. It is essential for professionals to familiarize themselves with the approved substitutes for R-22 that do not deplete the ozone layer, such as hydrofluorocarbons (HFCs) and newer alternatives like hydrofluoroolefins (HFOs).

Venting Prohibition During Servicing

The prohibition of venting refrigerants into the atmosphere during servicing activities is a critical component of the Clean Air Act regulations, aimed at minimizing the release of ozone-depleting substances and high global warming potential gases. This mandate requires that all technicians and service personnel involved in the maintenance, repair, or disposal of air conditioning and refrigeration equipment utilize approved refrigerant recovery and recycling equipment to capture and contain refrigerants rather than releasing them into the environment. The significance of this regulation cannot be overstated, as it directly addresses the prevention of further damage to the ozone layer and mitigates the impact of climate change by controlling the emission of potent greenhouse gases. In practical terms, the venting prohibition covers all refrigerants with ozone-depleting potential, including CFCs, HCFCs, and extends to their substitutes like HFCs, which, while not ozone-depleting, are potent greenhouse gases. The Environmental Protection Agency (EPA) enforces strict penalties for violations of this prohibition, underscoring the importance of compliance. Technicians must be certified under the EPA Section 608 and equipped with the knowledge and tools to properly recover refrigerants. This includes understanding the operation of recovery machines, the use of self-contained recovery equipment for different types of refrigerants, and the adherence to safety standards to prevent accidental releases during servicing.

Furthermore, the prohibition extends to specific practices during servicing, such as the mandatory evacuation of refrigerant to established recovery levels before opening equipment for maintenance or repair. This ensures that minimal refrigerant is released into the atmosphere and promotes the recycling and reuse of these substances, aligning with environmental sustainability goals. The EPA provides guidelines on the acceptable practices and procedures for refrigerant recovery, recycling, and reclamation, aiming to standardize the approach across the industry and ensure that all technicians are equipped to comply with the venting prohibition. To reinforce the importance of this regulation, the EPA mandates recordkeeping for the disposal of appliances containing refrigerants. Service companies and technicians must maintain detailed records of the quantity and type of refrigerant recovered, recycled, or reclaimed during servicing and disposal activities. This not only facilitates compliance checks but also promotes accountability within the industry, ensuring that all parties are contributing to the global effort to protect the environment.

The venting prohibition is a cornerstone of the EPA's strategy to phase out ozone-depleting substances and transition to more environmentally friendly refrigerants. It reflects a broader commitment to environmental stewardship and the responsible management of refrigerants throughout their lifecycle. For technicians and service personnel, adherence to this regulation is not only a legal obligation but also an ethical one, contributing to the protection of the ozone layer and the mitigation of climate change. As the HVACR industry continues to evolve, the importance of proper refrigerant management practices, including compliance with the venting prohibition, remains paramount, underscoring the collective responsibility to safeguard the environment for future generations.

Venting Prohibition at Disposal

The prohibition of venting refrigerants at the time of disposal is a critical measure under the Clean Air Act and is further supported by the Montreal Protocol to ensure the minimization of harmful emissions into the atmosphere. This regulation mandates that all refrigerants, whether they are CFCs, HCFCs, HFCs, or their substitutes, must be properly recovered and not released into the environment when disposing of air conditioning and refrigeration equipment. The significance of this requirement lies in its role in preventing the release of substances that have the potential to deplete the ozone layer or contribute to global warming. For HVACR professionals, this means that the process of disposing of equipment must include steps to recover refrigerants in accordance with EPA guidelines. The recovery of refrigerants is not only a legal requirement but also an ethical obligation to protect the environment from the potential harms associated with improper disposal practices. The EPA has established specific recovery techniques and equipment that must be used to ensure that refrigerants are contained and not vented into the atmosphere. This includes the use of EPA-certified recovery machines that are designed to safely remove refrigerants from equipment prior to disposal. Moreover, the EPA mandates that technicians who perform these recovery tasks must be certified under Section 608 of the Clean Air Act, demonstrating their knowledge and competency in handling refrigerants in a manner that complies with federal regulations. This certification process ensures that technicians are equipped with the necessary skills and understanding to properly manage refrigerants throughout their lifecycle, including the final stage of disposal.

In addition to the recovery of refrigerants, the EPA also requires detailed recordkeeping of the disposal process. This includes documenting the type and amount of refrigerant recovered, the method of recovery used, and the final disposition of the recovered refrigerant. These records serve as a means of accountability and compliance verification, ensuring that all parties involved in the disposal of refrigeration and air conditioning equipment adhere to the established regulations. The prohibition on venting refrigerants at disposal underscores the broader commitment to environmental protection and sustainability within the HVACR industry. By adhering to these regulations, professionals not only comply with legal requirements but also contribute to the global effort to protect the ozone layer and reduce the impact of climate change. The emphasis on proper refrigerant management practices, including the critical step of recovery at disposal, reflects the industry's role in fostering a more sustainable and environmentally responsible future.

Prohibition on Venting Refrigerants

The prohibition on venting substitute refrigerants into the atmosphere is a critical aspect of the Clean Air Act, reflecting the ongoing commitment to environmental protection. This regulation extends beyond traditional refrigerants to include substitutes that, while not directly depleting the ozone layer, may still contribute significantly to global warming if released. The Environmental Protection Agency (EPA) has identified that the responsible management of all refrigerants, including substitutes such as hydrofluorocarbons (HFCs) and hydrofluoroolefins (HFOs), is essential in the fight against climate change. The venting prohibition mandates that during the servicing, maintenance, repair, or disposal of HVACR equipment, all refrigerants must be properly recovered and contained rather than released into the environment. This directive underscores the importance of utilizing advanced recovery and recycling technologies that are capable of handling a wide range of refrigerants, including the latest substitutes. Technicians must be adept at operating such equipment, ensuring that the recovery process is both efficient and compliant with EPA regulations. The emphasis on preventing the release of substitute refrigerants aligns with broader environmental goals, including the reduction of greenhouse gas emissions and the promotion of sustainability within the HVACR industry.

Compliance with the venting prohibition requires a thorough understanding of the properties and handling requirements of substitute refrigerants. Technicians must be trained and certified under the EPA Section 608 program, which has been updated to include the management of these substitutes. This education ensures that HVACR professionals are equipped with the knowledge necessary to make informed decisions regarding the use, recovery, and disposal of all types of refrigerants.

The EPA's stringent approach to the regulation of substitute refrigerants through the venting prohibition is a testament to the evolving nature of environmental protection efforts. It highlights the necessity for the HVACR industry to adapt to new challenges and technologies, ensuring that the transition to environmentally friendly refrigerants does not compromise the overarching goal of reducing atmospheric pollutants. As the industry continues to innovate and embrace alternative refrigerants, the adherence to these regulations will play a pivotal role in safeguarding the environment for future generations, demonstrating a collective responsibility towards sustainable practices and the mitigation of climate change.

Maximum Penalty Under Clean Air Act

The Clean Air Act (CAA) enforces stringent penalties for non-compliance with its regulations, including those related to the venting, recovery, and recycling of refrigerants. These penalties are designed to deter violations and ensure adherence to practices that protect the environment from harmful emissions. The maximum penalty under the Clean Air Act can be substantial, reflecting the seriousness with which the Environmental Protection Agency (EPA) views violations of its regulations. For individuals or entities found in violation of the CAA provisions, fines can reach up to $37,500 per day for each violation. This amount is not static; it is subject to adjustments for inflation and can vary depending on the nature and severity of the infraction.

In addition to financial penalties, the EPA may also impose corrective measures requiring the violator to come into compliance within a specified timeframe. Failure to adhere to these corrective measures can result in further penalties or legal action. The EPA's enforcement of these penalties underscores the importance of compliance with the Clean Air Act and serves as a reminder to HVACR professionals of the legal and financial risks associated with non-compliance. It is crucial for technicians, service managers, and company owners in the HVACR industry to understand the implications of these penalties. Ensuring that all personnel are properly trained and certified under EPA Section 608 is a fundamental step in mitigating the risk of violations. Additionally, adopting best practices for refrigerant management, including the use of EPA-certified recovery and recycling equipment, can further safeguard against potential penalties. The emphasis on strict penalties highlights the EPA's commitment to environmental protection and the role of the HVACR industry in achieving these goals. By adhering to the regulations set forth in the Clean Air Act, professionals not only avoid significant financial and legal repercussions but also contribute to the broader effort to protect the ozone layer and combat climate change. This alignment with environmental objectives not only ensures compliance but also enhances the reputation and operational standards of those within the industry.

Montreal Protocol

The Montreal Protocol stands as a pivotal international agreement, aimed at phasing out the production and consumption of substances that deplete the ozone layer. This treaty, ratified by countries worldwide, underscores a collective commitment to environmental protection and the mitigation of ozone layer depletion. The protocol categorizes ozone-depleting substances (ODS) into several groups, each with its own timeline for phase-out, reflecting the varying degrees of harm they inflict on the stratospheric ozone layer. Among these substances, chlorofluorocarbons (CFCs), halons, and hydrochlorofluorocarbons (HCFCs) have been primary targets due to their high ozone depletion potential (ODP).

The phasedown approach adopted by the Montreal Protocol has been instrumental in the gradual reduction of ODS in the atmosphere. It sets forth a framework for developed and developing countries, acknowledging the differences in their starting points and capacities to transition away from ODS. Developed countries have led the phase-out, with binding commitments to reduce and eventually eliminate the use of these harmful substances. Developing countries, on the other hand, have been granted a grace period, allowing them more time to meet their phase-out obligations. This differentiation ensures that all parties can contribute to global efforts without compromising their developmental goals. The Montreal Protocol also established the Multilateral Fund, a financial mechanism designed to assist developing countries in meeting their protocol obligations. This fund supports various activities, including the transfer of technologies that are environmentally safe, capacity building, and the promotion of industry best practices. The success of the Multilateral Fund lies in its ability to facilitate cooperation between countries, industries, and non-governmental organizations, fostering a collaborative approach to environmental protection.

The impact of the Montreal Protocol is evident in the significant decrease in the production and consumption of ODS since its inception. Scientific assessments indicate a recovery of the ozone layer, projecting a return to pre-1980 levels by the middle of the 21st century, provided that the protocol's regulations continue to be strictly enforced. This positive trend underscores the effectiveness of international cooperation in addressing global environmental challenges. For HVACR professionals, understanding the implications of the Montreal Protocol is crucial. The transition to alternative refrigerants, such as hydrofluorocarbons (HFCs) and hydrofluoroolefins (HFOs), which have lower ODP and global warming potential (GWP), is a direct result of the protocol's mandates. Technicians must be adept at handling these substitutes, ensuring compliance with both domestic regulations and international agreements. The protocol's emphasis on proper refrigerant management, including recovery, recycling, and reclamation, aligns with the broader goal of sustainable environmental practices.

The Montreal Protocol serves as a testament to the global community's ability to unite in the face of environmental crises. Its ongoing evolution, including amendments and adjustments, reflects the dynamic nature of scientific understanding and technological advancement. The Kigali Amendment, for example, aims to address hydrofluorocarbons (HFCs), potent greenhouse gases not initially covered by the protocol, further exemplifying the agreement's adaptability and commitment to comprehensive environmental stewardship.

As the HVACR industry continues to navigate the transition to more environmentally friendly refrigerants and technologies, the principles and objectives of the Montreal Protocol remain central. The protocol not only guides regulatory frameworks and industry standards but also inspires innovation and progress toward a more sustainable future.

Section 608 Regulations

High and Low-Pressure Refrigerants

High and low-pressure refrigerants are classified based on their discharge pressure at a given operating temperature. This classification is critical for technicians to understand as it influences the choice of equipment, safety procedures, and compliance with environmental regulations. High-pressure refrigerants, such as R-410A, operate at pressures significantly above atmospheric pressure even at normal ambient temperatures. These refrigerants are commonly used in residential and commercial air conditioning systems due to their efficiency and lower ozone depletion potential compared to older refrigerants. On the other hand, low-pressure refrigerants, like R-123 and R-11, operate at pressures closer to atmospheric pressure and are typically found in large commercial and industrial chillers. The distinction between high and low-pressure refrigerants is not merely academic but has practical implications for handling, recovery, and leak detection.

Technicians must be adept at identifying the type of refrigerant in a system before performing any maintenance or repair work. This identification process involves checking the nameplate information on the equipment, which should list the type of refrigerant used, or using refrigerant identifiers. Proper identification is crucial to prevent the mixing of refrigerants, which can lead to system damage, reduced efficiency, and increased environmental harm. The Environmental Protection Agency (EPA) mandates specific recovery techniques and equipment for different pressure categories of refrigerants to minimize accidental releases and ensure safe handling. For instance, recovery machines used for high-pressure refrigerants are designed to withstand the higher pressures without leakage, whereas those intended for low-pressure refrigerants are equipped with features to prevent freezing or damage due to the lower pressure operation.

Understanding the pressure-temperature relationship is also fundamental when working with these refrigerants. This relationship helps technicians determine the correct operating pressures for a system and diagnose issues such as undercharging or overcharging of refrigerant. For high-pressure refrigerants, the pressure-temperature charts are essential tools for ensuring systems operate within safe and efficient parameters. Similarly, for low-pressure systems, knowing the saturation temperature at a given pressure allows for accurate leak detection and system diagnostics.

System-Dependent vs. Self-Contained Equipment

System-dependent recovery equipment, often referred to as passive recovery equipment, relies on the compressor of the air conditioning or refrigeration system to recover refrigerant. This type of equipment does not have its own means to draw refrigerant out of the system; instead, it utilizes the pressure differential created by the system's compressor or by manually creating a pressure differential. System-dependent methods are typically used for smaller applications, such as domestic refrigerators or small window air conditioners, where the amount of refrigerant is relatively low. The primary advantage of system-dependent recovery is its simplicity and cost-effectiveness. However, it is slower than using self-contained equipment and may not be suitable for larger systems or for situations where the system's compressor is non-functional.

On the other hand, self-contained recovery equipment, also known as active recovery equipment, has its own compressor or pump built into the unit to recover refrigerant. This type of equipment is capable of efficiently removing refrigerant from systems regardless of the operational status of the system's compressor. Self-contained units are designed to handle larger quantities of refrigerant and can be used across a wide range of system sizes, including commercial and industrial applications. These units are faster and more efficient at recovering refrigerant than system-dependent methods, making them the preferred choice for most professional HVACR technicians. Self-contained recovery equipment also typically includes features for filtering and removing moisture and contaminants from the refrigerant, which is crucial for both environmental protection and for maintaining the integrity of the refrigerant for reuse. The distinction between system-dependent and self-contained recovery equipment is critical for technicians to understand, as the choice of equipment affects the efficiency, speed, and environmental impact of refrigerant recovery operations. The Environmental Protection Agency (EPA) mandates the use of certified recovery equipment to ensure that refrigerant is recovered and recycled or disposed of properly, to minimize release into the atmosphere. Technicians must be trained and certified in proper recovery techniques and in the use of recovery equipment to comply with Section 608 regulations of the Clean Air Act.

Choosing the appropriate recovery equipment is not only a matter of regulatory compliance but also of professional competence. Technicians must assess the situation, including the type and size of the system, the condition of the system's compressor, and the amount of refrigerant to be recovered, to select the most effective recovery method. This decision-making process is crucial for ensuring the safety of the technician, the efficiency of the recovery operation, and the protection of the environment. In practice, the use of self-contained recovery equipment is often the most versatile and reliable method, suitable for a wide range of scenarios that HVACR technicians encounter. However, understanding when and how to use system-dependent recovery methods remains a valuable skill, particularly for working with smaller systems or in situations where the use of more sophisticated equipment may not be practical. The ability to effectively use both types of equipment, in accordance with EPA regulations and industry best practices, is a hallmark of skilled and responsible HVACR professionals.

Equipment Covered by the Rule

The rule encompasses a broad spectrum of air-conditioning and refrigeration equipment, specifically targeting those systems that utilize chlorofluorocarbons (CFCs) and hydrochlorofluorocarbons (HCFCs) as refrigerants. This directive is a critical component of the regulatory framework designed to mitigate environmental damage by controlling substances known to deplete the ozone layer. It is imperative for technicians to recognize that virtually all stationary refrigeration and air-conditioning systems fall within the purview of this regulation, with the notable exception of motor vehicle air conditioners. This exception is due to the distinct regulatory path that governs automotive systems, which are subject to separate standards and certification processes.

The equipment covered under this rule includes but is not limited to residential HVAC units, commercial refrigeration and freezer units, industrial cooling systems, and heat pumps. Each of these systems, when containing CFCs or HCFCs, must be serviced, maintained, and disposed of in accordance with the guidelines set forth to ensure minimal release of these ozone-depleting substances into the atmosphere. The rule's applicability to such a wide array of equipment underscores the EPA's comprehensive approach to ozone layer protection. It also highlights the importance of technician certification under Section 608, as these professionals play a direct role in the proper handling of refrigerants across the equipment's lifecycle. For technicians working in the field, understanding the specific types of equipment covered by the rule is fundamental. This knowledge not only ensures compliance with environmental regulations but also guides the selection of appropriate recovery, recycling, and disposal techniques. For instance, commercial refrigeration units often contain large quantities of HCFC-22 (R-22), a refrigerant with a higher ozone depletion potential than some of its alternatives. The proper recovery of R-22 during servicing or at the end of the unit's life is crucial to preventing its release into the atmosphere. Furthermore, the rule's distinction between equipment types extends to the certification levels required for technicians. Those working with systems covered by the rule must obtain EPA Section 608 certification, which is segmented into types that correspond to the size and complexity of the systems. This certification ensures that technicians have demonstrated proficiency in handling refrigerants in a manner that aligns with environmental safety standards.

In addition to stationary systems, the rule also addresses the requirements for refrigerant recovery and recycling equipment itself. Recovery and recycling units used in the servicing of air-conditioning and refrigeration equipment must be certified by the EPA, ensuring they meet efficiency and safety standards necessary for minimizing refrigerant release. This aspect of the rule further emphasizes the comprehensive strategy employed by the EPA to encompass all facets of refrigerant management, from the equipment being serviced to the tools used in its maintenance. Technicians must also be aware of the evolving nature of refrigerant use and regulation. As the HVACR industry moves towards refrigerants with lower global warming potential (GWP) and ozone depletion potential (ODP), the scope of equipment covered by regulatory rules may adjust accordingly. Staying informed about these changes is essential for maintaining compliance and supporting environmental protection efforts.

The identification of equipment covered by the rule is a critical step in ensuring that the objectives of the Clean Air Act and the Montreal Protocol are met. By adhering to these guidelines, technicians contribute to a global effort to protect the ozone layer and reduce the impact of climate change, underscoring the environmental and ethical obligations inherent in the HVACR profession.

Third-Party Certification for Recycling

The requirement for third-party certification of recycling and recovery equipment is a critical component of the Section 608 regulations under the Clean Air Act, aimed at ensuring the proper handling and disposal of refrigerants to minimize their environmental impact. This mandate underscores the importance of using equipment that meets stringent performance and safety standards, as certified by recognized testing organizations. The certification process involves rigorous testing and evaluation of recovery and recycling equipment to ensure they effectively remove refrigerants without releasing them into the atmosphere. This step is crucial for preventing the emission of ozone-depleting substances and greenhouse gases, which contribute to global warming and ozone layer depletion. Third-party certification provides an independent verification that the equipment complies with EPA standards, offering assurance to technicians and businesses about the reliability and environmental compliance of their operations. It is a testament to the equipment's capability to perform under various conditions, ensuring that refrigerants are recovered and recycled with minimal loss. The certification covers various aspects of equipment performance, including the efficiency of refrigerant recovery, the purity of the refrigerant after recycling, and the safety features that prevent accidental releases.

For HVACR technicians, understanding the significance of using certified equipment is paramount. It not only facilitates compliance with legal requirements but also enhances the credibility of their services among customers who are increasingly environmentally conscious. Technicians should verify the certification status of their equipment and stay informed about the latest standards and requirements. This knowledge is essential for selecting the right tools for the job, optimizing the recovery and recycling process, and making informed decisions about equipment investments. Manufacturers of recovery and recycling equipment also play a vital role in this ecosystem. They are responsible for ensuring their products undergo third-party certification and for keeping their certifications current. This involves continuous research and development to improve equipment efficiency, reduce its environmental footprint, and adapt to the evolving landscape of refrigerants and HVACR technologies. By investing in certified equipment, manufacturers contribute to the industry's overall efforts to protect the environment and promote sustainable practices.

The EPA provides a list of certified equipment, which is a valuable resource for technicians and businesses in the HVACR industry. This list helps in identifying equipment that has been tested and approved by authorized certification bodies, making it easier to comply with Section 608 regulations. Regular updates to this list reflect the dynamic nature of the industry, with new technologies and refrigerants being developed, requiring ongoing evaluation and certification. In addition to the environmental benefits, using certified recovery and recycling equipment can lead to operational efficiencies, reduced costs over time, and avoidance of penalties for non-compliance. It underscores the technician's role in environmental stewardship, aligning with the broader goals of the Clean Air Act and the Montreal Protocol to phase out ozone-depleting substances. The emphasis on third-party certification highlights a collective responsibility among technicians, businesses, and equipment manufacturers to uphold the highest standards of environmental protection.

Reclaimed Refrigerant Standard

The **Air Conditioning, Heating, and Refrigeration Institute (AHRI) Standard 700-2016** specifies the requirements for the purity of reclaimed refrigerants to ensure they meet or exceed the quality of new refrigerants. This standard is pivotal for HVACR technicians as it directly impacts the effectiveness and environmental compatibility of the refrigerants used in various systems. Reclaimed refrigerants are those that have been processed to remove contaminants and restore the refrigerant to a condition that meets the specifications for new refrigerant gases. The process of reclaiming not only extends the life cycle of refrigerants but also plays a crucial role in reducing the environmental impact associated with the production of new refrigerants.

The AHRI Standard 700-2016 outlines the acceptable levels of non-condensable gases, moisture, acidity, and high-boiling residue in reclaimed refrigerants. For technicians, understanding these specifications is essential for ensuring that the refrigerants they use or recommend meet the stringent requirements set forth for system efficiency and environmental safety. The standard also includes test methods for verifying the purity of reclaimed refrigerants, providing a clear protocol for third-party certification bodies to assess the quality of refrigerants before they re-enter the market. Compliance with AHRI Standard 700-2016 is not just about adhering to regulations; it's about contributing to a larger effort to protect the ozone layer and combat climate change. By utilizing reclaimed refrigerants that meet these high standards, technicians can assure their clients of the operational integrity of their HVACR systems while also demonstrating a commitment to environmental stewardship. The standard serves as a benchmark for quality, ensuring that all stakeholders in the HVACR industry—from manufacturers to end-users—have a common understanding of what constitutes a reclaimed refrigerant that is safe, effective, and environmentally responsible. For HVACR professionals, familiarizing themselves with the specifics of AHRI Standard 700-2016 is an investment in their practice and the planet. It underscores the importance of choosing suppliers and reclaimers who adhere to this standard, thereby supporting a sustainable approach to refrigerant management. As the industry continues to evolve, the role of standards like AHRI 700-2016 in promoting best practices and environmental sustainability remains indispensable.

The Sales Restriction

The sales restriction, as mandated by the Environmental Protection Agency (EPA) under Section 608 of the Clean Air Act, plays a pivotal role in ensuring that refrigerants are handled and distributed by certified professionals only. This regulation is designed to prevent the release of ozone-depleting substances (ODS) and substitutes into the atmosphere by restricting the sale of certain refrigerants to individuals who have not obtained the appropriate EPA certification. The restriction covers refrigerants that are found in household and commercial refrigeration systems, air conditioning units, and other equipment that relies on these substances for cooling purposes. The primary goal of this restriction is to ensure that those who purchase, handle, and work with these refrigerants have the necessary knowledge and skills to do so in a manner that minimizes environmental impact and adheres to safety standards.

Under the sales restriction, wholesalers and retailers are required to verify the certification status of individuals purchasing refrigerants. This verification process involves checking the EPA certification credentials of the buyer to ensure they are authorized to handle the type of refrigerant being sold. The restriction applies to all refrigerants that have been identified as having the potential to harm the ozone layer, including but not limited to chlorofluorocarbons (CFCs), hydrochlorofluorocarbons (HCFCs), and any blend containing one or more of these substances. It is important to note that the sales restriction also extends to refrigerant-containing products, such as air conditioning and refrigeration equipment pre-charged with restricted refrigerants.

The enforcement of the sales restriction is critical for the success of the EPA's efforts to phase out ozone-depleting substances and transition to more environmentally friendly alternatives. By limiting access to these substances, the EPA aims to reduce unauthorized releases during servicing, maintenance, repair, and disposal of refrigeration and air-conditioning equipment. The regulation also serves to encourage proper recovery, recycling, and reclaiming practices among certified technicians, further supporting environmental protection efforts. To comply with the sales restriction, certified technicians must maintain their credentials and be prepared to present them upon request when purchasing refrigerants. Wholesalers, retailers, and other suppliers are responsible for maintaining records of refrigerant sales, including information about the buyer's certification status. These records are subject to inspection by the EPA to ensure compliance with the regulation.

The impact of the sales restriction extends beyond regulatory compliance and environmental protection. It also influences the professional development and market dynamics within the HVACR industry. By requiring certification for refrigerant purchases, the regulation promotes a higher standard of professionalism and expertise among technicians. This, in turn, can lead to improved service quality, enhanced system efficiency, and increased customer trust. Additionally, the restriction supports the market transition towards alternative refrigerants with lower ozone depletion and global warming potentials, driving innovation and adoption of new technologies in the HVACR sector. For individuals pursuing a career in the HVACR industry, understanding the sales restriction and its implications is essential. It not only affects day-to-day operations but also reflects a broader commitment to environmental stewardship and professional integrity. As the industry continues to evolve in response to environmental challenges and technological advancements, the role of certified technicians in ensuring safe and sustainable refrigerant management remains a cornerstone of efforts to protect the ozone layer and mitigate climate change.

Clean Air Act Venting Prohibition

The Clean Air Act, a pivotal piece of environmental legislation in the United States, strictly prohibits the venting of refrigerants into the atmosphere. This prohibition is a critical component of the Act's broader aim to protect the stratospheric ozone layer and combat climate change. Refrigerants, particularly those classified as CFCs, HCFCs, and even HFCs, possess significant ozone-depleting potential (ODP) and global warming potential (GWP). The Act categorically bans the release of these substances during the servicing, maintenance, repair, or disposal of air conditioning and refrigeration equipment.

The prohibition on venting is enforced through stringent regulations that mandate the recovery, recycling, or reclaiming of refrigerants. Technicians working with HVACR systems are required to use certified recovery equipment to ensure that refrigerants are not released into the atmosphere. The EPA Section 608 regulations outline specific practices for the handling of refrigerants, including the certification requirements for technicians and the standards for recovery equipment.

Violations of the venting prohibition can result in substantial penalties, underscoring the seriousness with which the EPA regards this issue. The maximum penalty under the Clean Air Act reflects the potential environmental harm caused by the release of ozone-depleting substances. It serves as a deterrent against non-compliance and emphasizes the importance of adhering to environmentally responsible refrigerant management practices. In addition to the environmental implications, the venting prohibition has significant implications for HVACR technicians and businesses. Compliance with the regulations requires an understanding of the proper techniques for refrigerant recovery, recycling, and reclaiming. Technicians must be proficient in the use of recovery equipment and familiar with the types of refrigerants they are handling. This knowledge is not only crucial for passing the EPA 608 certification exam but also for ensuring the safety and efficiency of HVACR systems.

The prohibition on venting is a key element of the EPA's efforts to phase out ozone-depleting substances and transition to more environmentally friendly refrigerants. The development and adoption of substitute refrigerants with lower ODP and GWP are part of this broader strategy. However, the compatibility of these substitutes with existing lubricants and equipment presents additional challenges for technicians. Understanding the properties and requirements of substitute refrigerants is essential for maintaining compliance with the Clean Air Act and ensuring the continued effectiveness of the HVACR industry's contribution to environmental protection. As the HVACR industry evolves, the importance of adhering to the Clean Air Act's venting prohibition remains paramount. It is a fundamental aspect of the professional responsibilities of HVACR technicians and a critical component of the industry's role in environmental stewardship.

Substitute Refrigerants and Oils

Absence of Refrigerants

The transition to substitute refrigerants and oils in the HVACR industry is a critical step towards reducing the environmental impact of refrigeration and air conditioning systems. These substitutes are designed to have lower ozone depletion potential (ODP) and global warming potential (GWP) compared to traditional refrigerants like CFCs and HCFCs. However, the shift also introduces challenges related to compatibility and system efficiency. Many substitute refrigerants cannot be used with the mineral oil lubricants that are compatible with older refrigerants. Instead, they require synthetic lubricants such as polyolester (POE) oils, which offer better miscibility and stability with these newer refrigerants. One significant issue that arises with the use of substitute refrigerants is the potential for fractionation. This phenomenon occurs when a refrigerant blend leaks from a system at different rates due to the varying volatilities of its components. Fractionation can alter the composition of the refrigerant remaining in the system, potentially affecting system performance and complicating the process of charging and servicing the equipment. To mitigate these issues, technicians must be well-versed in the properties of both the substitute refrigerants and their compatible lubricants. They must also be adept at identifying and addressing leaks promptly to maintain system integrity and performance.

Furthermore, the introduction of substitute refrigerants necessitates an update in the training and certification of HVACR technicians. Understanding the thermodynamic properties of these substitutes, as well as the proper handling and recovery techniques, is essential for maintaining compliance with environmental regulations and ensuring the safe operation of refrigeration and air conditioning systems. The EPA 608 certification exam has been updated to include information on these substitutes, reflecting the industry's move towards more sustainable practices. In addressing the challenges associated with substitute refrigerants and oils, the HVACR industry is taking a significant step forward in environmental stewardship. By equipping technicians with the knowledge and skills needed to work with these substitutes, the industry ensures a smoother transition to greener alternatives, ultimately contributing to the global effort to protect the ozone layer and reduce greenhouse gas emissions.

Refrigerant and Lubricant Incompatibility

The transition to environmentally friendly refrigerants necessitates a comprehensive understanding of the compatibility between these substitutes and the lubricants used within refrigeration and air conditioning systems. The incompatibility issues stem from the chemical properties of the refrigerants and the lubricants, which can affect the efficiency and longevity of HVACR systems. For instance, traditional CFC and HCFC refrigerants were commonly used with mineral oil lubricants due to their mutual solubility and stability. However, with the shift towards hydrofluorocarbon (HFC) refrigerants, such as **R-134a**, and hydrofluoroolefins (HFOs), the industry has had to adapt by using synthetic lubricants like polyolester (POE) oils. These synthetic lubricants are designed to be compatible with the newer refrigerants, offering improved miscibility and stability, which are crucial for the efficient operation of modern refrigeration systems. The compatibility between refrigerants and lubricants is not just a matter of operational efficiency; it also impacts the environmental performance of the refrigeration system. Incompatible combinations can lead to increased energy consumption and, consequently, higher greenhouse gas emissions. Furthermore, leakage of refrigerants due to incompatibility issues not only contributes to ozone depletion and global warming but also results in higher operational costs due to the need for more frequent maintenance and refrigerant replenishment.

For technicians working in the HVACR industry, understanding the specific lubricants required for different refrigerants is essential. **Polyolester (POE) oils** are widely used with HFCs and HFOs due to their compatibility and performance characteristics. However, when dealing with HCFCs, such as **R-22**, technicians may encounter systems that still use **alkylbenzene lubricants**. These lubricants offer a degree of compatibility with both HCFCs and some HFCs, providing a transitional solution for systems undergoing retrofitting from HCFCs to HFCs or HFOs. It is crucial for technicians to be aware of the refrigerant-lubricant combinations that are approved by manufacturers and adhere to these specifications to avoid system failures and ensure compliance with environmental regulations. The issue of lubricant-refrigerant compatibility extends beyond the choice of lubricant type. Technicians must also consider the potential for **fractionation** in refrigerant blends, which can complicate the selection of appropriate lubricants. Fractionation refers to the separation of components in a refrigerant blend, which can occur due to differences in the volatilities of the blend's constituents. This separation can alter the chemical composition of the refrigerant within the system, potentially affecting its compatibility with the lubricant and the overall performance of the system. To address this challenge, technicians must select lubricants that maintain compatibility across the range of potential compositions resulting from fractionation.

Fractionation and Component Leakage

The phenomenon of **fractionation** in refrigerant blends poses a significant challenge in the HVACR industry, particularly when it comes to maintaining system efficiency and environmental compliance. This issue arises because the different components of a refrigerant blend have varying volatilities, leading to a situation where these components can leak from the system at different rates. Such differential leakage alters the composition of the refrigerant remaining in the system, which can have profound effects on both system performance and the environment. The altered composition may not only reduce the efficiency of the refrigeration cycle but also increase the system's operational costs due to the need for more frequent adjustments or refills of the refrigerant blend to restore its original composition.

Technicians must be acutely aware of the implications of fractionation, especially when servicing equipment that utilizes blended refrigerants. It is crucial to ensure that the refrigerant blend's composition remains as close to its original specification as possible to maintain optimal system performance and to adhere to environmental regulations. This requires a thorough understanding of the properties of the refrigerant blend, as well as the ability to detect and rectify leaks promptly. Moreover, when recharging a system with a refrigerant blend, technicians must take care to introduce the refrigerant in a manner that minimizes the risk of altering its composition. This often involves following specific procedures recommended by the refrigerant manufacturer, such as charging in a liquid state to ensure a consistent blend ratio. In addition to the operational challenges posed by fractionation, there are significant environmental concerns. Refrigerant blends are often designed to minimize ozone depletion potential (ODP) and global warming potential (GWP). However, if fractionation occurs and alters the blend's composition, these environmental benefits can be compromised. The leakage of components with higher ODP or GWP can contribute more significantly to environmental damage, undermining the purpose of using these blends. Therefore, managing the fractionation problem is not only a matter of maintaining system efficiency but also of upholding the HVACR industry's commitment to environmental stewardship.

To address these challenges, the industry has developed various strategies, including the use of advanced leak detection technologies that can identify leaks more quickly and accurately, allowing for prompt repairs. Additionally, the development of refrigerant blends that are less prone to fractionation represents an ongoing area of research and innovation. These efforts are complemented by the continuous education and training of HVACR technicians, ensuring they are equipped with the latest knowledge and skills to manage the complexities of working with refrigerant blends effectively.

The management of fractionation and component leakage is a critical aspect of modern refrigerant technology, requiring a comprehensive approach that encompasses proper system design, meticulous maintenance practices, and ongoing technician education. By addressing these issues effectively, the HVACR industry can ensure the continued efficiency and environmental performance of refrigeration and air conditioning systems, aligning with both regulatory requirements and sustainability goals.

Refrigeration

Refrigerant States and Pressures

Understanding the refrigeration cycle is crucial for HVACR technicians, as it forms the backbone of air conditioning and refrigeration systems. The cycle can be broken down into four main stages: evaporation, compression, condensation, and expansion. At each stage, the refrigerant undergoes various changes in state and pressure that are essential for the cooling process.

During the evaporation stage, the refrigerant is in a low-pressure, low-temperature liquid form. As it absorbs heat from the environment (e.g., the interior of a refrigerator or a room), it evaporates and transforms into a vapor. This phase change occurs because the refrigerant has a boiling point lower than the temperature of the environment from which it is absorbing heat. The vaporization of the refrigerant is what actually removes heat from the space being cooled, effectively lowering the temperature.

Following evaporation, the refrigerant vapor is drawn into the compressor. The compressor increases the pressure of the vapor, which in turn raises its temperature. The high-pressure, high-temperature vapor is then pushed into the condenser. It is in the condenser that the refrigerant releases the absorbed heat to the outside environment. As the refrigerant loses heat, it condenses back into a liquid form. However, this liquid is still under high pressure after leaving the condenser. The next step involves the expansion valve or device, which plays a critical role in the refrigeration cycle. As the high-pressure liquid refrigerant passes through the expansion valve, its pressure drops abruptly. This sudden reduction in pressure lowers the temperature of the refrigerant, cooling it significantly. The refrigerant is now ready to enter the evaporator, where it will once again absorb heat and evaporate, continuing the cycle.

The efficiency of the refrigeration cycle is heavily dependent on the properties of the refrigerant used, including its boiling point, heat of vaporization, and pressure-temperature relationship. These properties determine how effectively a refrigerant can absorb heat and transition between liquid and vapor states under varying conditions of pressure and temperature. Technicians must be adept at monitoring the pressures and temperatures at different points in the refrigeration cycle to diagnose and troubleshoot issues. For instance, excessive superheat (the temperature of the vapor refrigerant exiting the evaporator) can indicate a low refrigerant charge or a clogged expansion valve. Conversely, insufficient superheat may suggest an overcharged system or a malfunctioning compressor. Similarly, understanding the subcooling (the temperature difference between the liquid refrigerant in the condenser and its saturation temperature) can help identify issues with the condenser performance or refrigerant charge.

Refrigeration Gauges Usage and Codes

Understanding the proper use of refrigeration gauges is crucial for HVACR technicians to accurately diagnose and service refrigeration systems. These gauges, integral to the manifold gauge set, are designed to read the pressure of refrigerants within the system, providing vital data for troubleshooting and maintenance. The color coding of refrigeration gauges aids technicians in quickly identifying the high-pressure and low-pressure gauges: the high-pressure gauge is typically marked with red and the low-pressure gauge with blue. This color scheme is standardized to minimize confusion and ensure safety during use. The high-pressure gauge (red) measures the pressure of the refrigerant as it exits the compressor and enters the condenser, displaying readings in pounds per square inch (psi). The low-pressure gauge (blue), on the other hand, measures suction line pressure or the pressure of the refrigerant as it returns to the compressor from the evaporator. It's essential to note that the pressure readings on these gauges can vary significantly depending on the type of refrigerant used in the system. For instance, R-22, an HCFC refrigerant, operates at different pressures compared to R-410A, an HFC refrigerant, necessitating careful attention to the specific refrigerant's pressure-temperature chart for accurate diagnosis. Proper use of refrigeration gauges also involves ensuring they are correctly attached to the system's service ports, with the high-pressure gauge connected to the high side of the system and the low-pressure gauge to the low side. Before attaching the gauges, technicians must ensure they are zeroed out to avoid false readings. After securing the gauges, observing the system's pressure can provide insights into its operational status, such as indicating if the system is undercharged or overcharged with refrigerant or if there are restrictions in the refrigerant flow. In addition to pressure readings, some refrigeration gauges are equipped with temperature scales that allow technicians to calculate superheat and subcooling, further aiding in the diagnosis of refrigeration system issues. This dual functionality underscores the importance of familiarity with the gauge set's features and the refrigerant's properties to effectively interpret the readings and make informed decisions during servicing and troubleshooting.

Leak Detection

Leak detection in refrigeration systems is a critical skill for HVACR technicians, as even minor leaks can lead to significant losses in efficiency, increased operating costs, and potential environmental harm due to the release of refrigerants. The first step in effective leak detection is understanding the common signs of refrigerant leaks. These can include visible oil residue around refrigeration components, unexplained loss in cooling capacity, or fluctuations in system pressure readings that do not align with normal operational parameters. Technicians must be adept at using a variety of tools and techniques to identify the precise location of leaks, as the source can often be hidden or not immediately apparent.

One of the primary methods employed for leak detection is the use of electronic leak detectors, which are designed to sense the presence of refrigerants in the air. These devices are highly sensitive and can detect even small concentrations of refrigerant, making them invaluable for early detection of leaks. However, it's crucial for technicians to regularly calibrate these instruments and understand their specific detection limits, as different models may vary in sensitivity and the types of refrigerants they can detect. Another common technique involves the use of ultraviolet (UV) dye, which is added to the refrigerant. When the system is operated, the dye escapes with the refrigerant at the leak points and can be made visible under UV light, providing a clear indication of the leak's location. This method is particularly useful for finding multiple leaks or leaks in areas that are difficult to access or inspect visually. Soap bubble solutions represent a simpler, yet effective approach for identifying leaks. By applying the solution to suspected leak points and observing for bubble formation, technicians can pinpoint the exact location of a leak. This method is straightforward and cost-effective, making it a popular choice for routine maintenance and inspection tasks. It's important for technicians to understand the environmental implications of refrigerant leaks. Refrigerants such as CFCs, HCFCs, and even HFCs, though less harmful, can contribute to global warming and ozone depletion if released into the atmosphere. The EPA's regulations under Section 608 of the Clean Air Act mandate the proper handling, recovery, and recycling of refrigerants to minimize environmental impact. Compliance with these regulations not only protects the environment but also ensures the safety and efficiency of refrigeration systems.

In addition to environmental concerns, technicians must also be aware of the potential for refrigerant leaks to impact system performance and reliability. A leak can lead to reduced cooling capacity, increased energy consumption, and, ultimately, system failure if not addressed promptly. Regular leak detection and maintenance are essential for ensuring the longevity and efficiency of refrigeration systems, highlighting the importance of skilled technicians who are well-versed in the latest leak detection methods and technologies. To further enhance the accuracy of leak detection, technicians often resort to halide torches for systems still using HCFCs or CFCs. This method involves passing air from around the refrigeration components through a flame; if halogenated refrigerants are present, the flame will change color. While effective for certain types of refrigerants, this technique requires careful handling due to the use of an open flame and is less suitable for detecting leaks of non-halogenated refrigerants like HFCs. Nitrogen pressure testing is another critical technique, especially for detecting leaks in newly installed or repaired systems before they are charged with refrigerant. By pressurizing the system with nitrogen—a non-flammable, non-reactive gas—technicians can listen for escaping gas or use electronic or ultrasonic leak detectors to identify the leak location. This method is highly effective for ensuring system integrity and is an essential step in the commissioning process of HVACR systems. For comprehensive leak detection, technicians may also employ refrigerant recovery machines in conjunction with electronic detectors. By recovering the refrigerant and pressurizing the system with a trace amount of refrigerant mixed with nitrogen, technicians can enhance the sensitivity of electronic leak detectors. This approach combines the benefits of nitrogen pressure testing with the enhanced detection capabilities of electronic sensors, offering a robust solution for identifying leaks with precision.

Understanding the nuances of each leak detection method is crucial for technicians. Factors such as the type of refrigerant used, the system's age and condition, and the environmental conditions in which the system operates can all influence the choice of leak detection technique. Technicians must also stay informed about advancements in leak detection technology and the evolving regulations governing refrigerant use and handling. Continuous education and hands-on experience are key to mastering these techniques and ensuring that refrigeration systems are maintained in compliance with environmental and safety standards.

The role of HVACR technicians in managing and preventing refrigerant leaks cannot be overstated. Through diligent application of leak detection methods, technicians safeguard the environment, ensure system efficiency, and uphold the health and safety standards critical to the industry. As the HVACR field continues to evolve, the importance of skilled, knowledgeable technicians in maintaining the integrity and performance of refrigeration systems remains paramount.

Three R Definitions

Recover

The process of **recovering refrigerant** is a critical component in the maintenance, servicing, and disposal of HVACR systems, ensuring that these substances are not released into the atmosphere, where they can contribute to ozone depletion and global warming. The Environmental Protection Agency (EPA) mandates specific recovery techniques and procedures that HVACR technicians must follow, underscoring the importance of this process in environmental protection efforts. Recovery involves the safe extraction of refrigerants from systems into approved containers for the purpose of recycling, reclaiming, or proper disposal. This process not only prevents the release of harmful gases but also allows for the reuse of refrigerants, thereby reducing the need for the production of new refrigerants and the potential environmental impact associated with their manufacture. Technicians must be equipped with EPA-certified recovery equipment that is appropriate for the type of refrigerant being recovered. The selection of recovery equipment is crucial, as it must be capable of efficiently removing refrigerant without causing damage to the system or posing a risk to the technician. The equipment used is typically categorized based on the type of refrigerant and the pressure of the system from which the refrigerant is being recovered. For instance, systems containing **CFCs, HCFCs,** and **HFCs** require different recovery approaches and equipment specifications, including but not limited to, recovery tanks rated for the specific pressures of the refrigerants being handled.

The recovery process begins with the technician ensuring that the recovery equipment is properly connected to the HVACR system, with hoses attached to both the low and high sides of the system to facilitate the removal of refrigerant. The equipment must be checked for leaks to prevent the escape of refrigerant during the recovery process. Once the setup is verified to be secure and leak-free, the recovery machine is activated, and the refrigerant is extracted from the system. The speed and efficiency of recovery can be affected by various factors, including the ambient temperature, the condition of the recovery equipment, and the type and amount of refrigerant being recovered. Technicians must monitor the process closely, ensuring that the recovery equipment is functioning correctly and that the refrigerant is being collected into the recovery cylinder without release into the environment. After the recovery process is complete, the technician must ensure that the refrigerant is stored properly in recovery cylinders that are clearly labeled with the type of refrigerant they contain. These cylinders must be handled with care to avoid any damage or leaks, and they must be stored in a cool, dry place away from direct sunlight and sources of heat. The recovered refrigerant can then be sent to a certified reclamation facility where it is processed and purified for reuse, or it can be disposed of in accordance with EPA regulations if it is contaminated or no longer viable for use.

The significance of the recovery process extends beyond compliance with EPA regulations. It represents a commitment to environmental stewardship and the responsible management of resources. By recovering refrigerants effectively, technicians play a key role in minimizing the HVACR industry's impact on the planet, contributing to the reduction of greenhouse gas emissions and the protection of the ozone layer. This process also underscores the importance of technical skill, knowledge, and adherence to best practices in the field, as the proper handling of refrigerants is essential for both environmental protection and the safety of technicians and the public. As the HVACR industry continues to evolve, with new refrigerants and technologies emerging, the principles of refrigerant recovery remain a cornerstone of environmental responsibility and professional practice.

Recycle

Recycling refrigerants is a critical aspect of the HVACR industry's commitment to environmental stewardship and regulatory compliance. This process involves cleaning used refrigerant to a level that meets or exceeds industry standards for new refrigerant, without necessarily undergoing the more rigorous processes of reclamation. The Environmental Protection Agency (EPA) has established specific guidelines and requirements for recycling refrigerants, aiming to reduce the release of harmful substances into the atmosphere and promote the reuse of these materials in a manner that is safe and effective.

The recycling process typically takes place on-site and involves the use of specialized equipment designed to remove contaminants such as oil, moisture, acids, and other non-condensable gases from the refrigerant. This equipment must be EPA-certified and operated by technicians who have undergone proper training and certification under Section 608 of the Clean Air Act. The goal of recycling is to restore the refrigerant to a condition that is suitable for its intended use, which can significantly extend the life of the refrigerant and reduce the need for producing new materials. Technicians play a pivotal role in the recycling process, as their expertise and attention to detail ensure that the refrigerant is handled correctly and that the recycling equipment is maintained and operated according to EPA standards. They must carefully monitor the recycling process, ensuring that the refrigerant is not only cleaned of contaminants but also that it does not become cross-contaminated with other types of refrigerants. Cross-contamination can render the refrigerant unusable and may lead to system inefficiencies or failures if reintroduced into an HVACR system.

It is essential for technicians to document the recycling process meticulously, maintaining records of the quantity of refrigerant recycled, the type of refrigerant, and the equipment used. This documentation is crucial for compliance with EPA regulations and can also provide valuable information for managing refrigerant inventories and planning future recycling operations. By adhering to EPA guidelines and employing best practices for recycling refrigerants, HVACR technicians contribute to the sustainability of the industry and the protection of the environment. Recycling not only conserves valuable resources but also supports the overall goal of reducing greenhouse gas emissions and preserving the ozone layer, aligning with the industry's commitment to environmental responsibility and the well-being of future generations.

Reclaim

Refrigerant reclaiming is a process that goes beyond the basic removal of contaminants found in recycling. It involves restoring the refrigerant to its original purity and performance specifications, as defined by the Air Conditioning, Heating, and Refrigeration Institute (AHRI) Standard 700-2016. This standard specifies the requirements for the purity of reclaimed refrigerant, ensuring that it meets or exceeds the purity levels of new refrigerant. The reclaiming process is critical for the HVACR industry, as it allows for the safe and effective reuse of refrigerants, thereby reducing the environmental impact associated with the production of new refrigerants and the potential release of harmful substances into the atmosphere. The process of reclaiming refrigerants is carried out by EPA-certified reclamation facilities that have the necessary equipment and technology to purify refrigerants to the required standards. These facilities employ sophisticated procedures, including but not limited to, multiple filtration, distillation, and chemical treatment methods to remove impurities such as moisture, acids, oils, and other particulates from the refrigerant. The reclaimed refrigerant is then rigorously tested to ensure compliance with AHRI Standard 700-2016 before it can be certified for reuse in HVACR systems.

For HVACR technicians, understanding the distinction between recycled and reclaimed refrigerant is crucial. While recycled refrigerant is cleaned using on-site equipment for immediate reuse within the same system or facility, reclaimed refrigerant undergoes a more thorough purification process and is certified by an EPA-approved reclamation facility for use in any system. This distinction underscores the importance of proper labeling and documentation when handling refrigerants, as it ensures the traceability and legality of the refrigerant's use according to EPA regulations.

Technicians must also be aware of the environmental benefits of refrigerant reclaiming. By participating in the reclaiming process, they contribute to the reduction of greenhouse gas emissions and help protect the ozone layer. Moreover, reclaiming extends the life cycle of refrigerants, promoting sustainability within the HVACR industry. As the industry continues to evolve, with a growing emphasis on environmental responsibility, the role of refrigerant reclaiming will become increasingly significant, highlighting the need for technicians to stay informed about best practices and regulatory requirements related to refrigerant management.

Recovery Techniques

Avoid Mixing Refrigerants

Avoiding the mixing of refrigerants is crucial for maintaining system efficiency, ensuring safety, and complying with legal and environmental regulations. When different refrigerants are mixed, it can lead to a reduction in the overall efficiency of the HVACR system, potentially causing damage to the compressor and other components due to incompatible pressures and temperatures. Moreover, mixed refrigerants can complicate the recovery and recycling process, making it difficult to reclaim the refrigerant to purity standards required by the EPA. To prevent the mixing of refrigerants, technicians must use dedicated recovery cylinders for each type of refrigerant. This practice eliminates the risk of cross-contamination and ensures that the recovered refrigerant can be properly recycled or reclaimed. Additionally, clearly labeling each cylinder with the type of refrigerant it contains is essential to avoid any confusion during the recovery process.

Technicians should also use refrigerant identifiers before recovery to confirm the type of refrigerant in the system. This step is vital in situations where the existing labeling on the equipment might be missing or unclear. Identifying the refrigerant before proceeding ensures that the correct recovery procedures are followed and that the refrigerant is not inadvertently mixed with others in the recovery cylinder. In cases where mixed refrigerants are discovered, it is important to follow EPA guidelines for the disposal of contaminated refrigerants. These refrigerants cannot be recycled or reclaimed and must be handled as hazardous waste according to federal and state regulations. The disposal process should be documented thoroughly to maintain compliance with environmental laws. By adhering to these practices, technicians can avoid the pitfalls associated with mixing refrigerants, ensuring the longevity and efficiency of HVACR systems while upholding environmental and safety standards.

Factors Affecting Recovery Speed

Ambient temperature plays a significant role in the speed of refrigerant recovery. Higher temperatures can increase the pressure inside the refrigerant container, facilitating a quicker transfer of refrigerant from the HVAC system to the recovery unit. Conversely, lower temperatures may slow down the process by reducing the pressure differential, necessitating more time to achieve complete recovery. Technicians should consider the ambient temperature when planning recovery operations and adjust their methods accordingly to ensure efficiency.

The size of recycling or recovery equipment also impacts the speed of recovery. Larger equipment typically has a higher capacity for refrigerant recovery, enabling faster removal of refrigerants from systems. This is particularly important in commercial settings where systems contain large quantities of refrigerants. Selecting the appropriate size of recovery equipment for the job is crucial to optimize the recovery process and minimize downtime. Hose length and diameter are additional factors that affect the speed of recovery. Shorter hoses with larger diameters can reduce resistance and allow for a quicker flow of refrigerant, speeding up the recovery process. In contrast, longer hoses or those with smaller diameters can restrict refrigerant flow, leading to longer recovery times. Technicians should use the shortest and widest hoses that are practical for the job to enhance recovery efficiency. Understanding these factors is essential for HVACR technicians to perform refrigerant recovery efficiently and effectively.

Dehydration Evacuation

Evacuating Systems for Air and Moisture Removal

Evacuating systems to remove air and moisture is a critical step in ensuring the longevity and efficiency of HVACR systems. Air in the system can lead to non-condensable gases which reduce cooling capacity and efficiency, while moisture can cause corrosion, freeze-up, and even the breakdown of the refrigerant oil, leading to system failure. Therefore, it is imperative that technicians meticulously follow procedures for system evacuation to achieve a deep vacuum, effectively removing air and moisture from the system. The process begins with the proper connection of the vacuum pump to the system, ensuring that all valves are open and the system is secure. Using a high-quality vacuum pump is essential as it needs to achieve a vacuum level sufficient to boil off moisture at room temperature, typically around 500 microns or lower. It is crucial to monitor the vacuum with a reliable micron gauge, as relying solely on the vacuum pump's gauge may not provide an accurate reading of the vacuum level within the system.

Technicians must be patient during this process, as rushing can lead to incomplete removal of moisture and air, compromising the system's integrity. The duration of the evacuation process depends on several factors, including the size of the system, the amount of moisture present, and the ambient temperature. In some cases, especially for larger systems or those with significant moisture, applying a heat source to the system can expedite the process by increasing the vapor pressure of the water, making it easier to remove. Once the desired vacuum level is achieved, it is critical to perform an isolation test to ensure there are no leaks. This involves closing the valve between the vacuum pump and the system and observing the micron gauge for any increase in pressure. An increase indicates a potential leak or that moisture is still present and boiling off, requiring further evacuation. After successfully evacuating the system, the next step is to charge it with refrigerant. This must be done carefully to avoid introducing air or moisture back into the system. Charging with refrigerant should be done through the use of a charging cylinder or scale to ensure the correct amount of refrigerant is added, based on the manufacturer's specifications.

Safety

Refrigerant Exposure Risks

Exposure to refrigerants poses significant health risks that HVACR technicians must be acutely aware of to ensure their safety and that of those around them. **Oxygen deprivation** is a critical concern, especially in confined spaces where refrigerant gases, heavier than air, can accumulate and displace oxygen, leading to asphyxiation. This risk underscores the importance of adequate ventilation in work areas and the use of oxygen sensors to detect unsafe oxygen levels. **Cardiac effects** are another serious risk associated with certain refrigerants, such as R-123, which can sensitize the heart to adrenaline, leading to irregular heart rhythms or even cardiac arrest following high-level exposure. This potential hazard highlights the need for technicians to use personal protective equipment (PPE) and follow safe handling procedures to minimize exposure.

Frostbite is a risk when handling refrigerants, particularly during the transfer of liquid refrigerant, which can rapidly evaporate and cool, causing severe cold burns on contact with skin. Wearing gloves and eye protection is essential to prevent direct contact with refrigerants and protect against frostbite and eye damage. Long-term exposure to refrigerants can lead to chronic health issues, including organ damage and reproductive effects, emphasizing the need for adherence to exposure limits and the use of PPE to mitigate these risks. Technicians must be trained to recognize the symptoms of refrigerant exposure, such as dizziness, shortness of breath, and palpitations, and to respond promptly to exposure incidents by seeking fresh air and medical evaluation. Understanding the specific risks associated with different types of refrigerants and implementing safety measures, such as proper ventilation, use of refrigerant detectors, and adherence to safety protocols, are crucial for minimizing the health risks posed by refrigerant exposure. This knowledge not only ensures the safety and well-being of HVACR professionals but also aligns with environmental and regulatory standards aimed at protecting individuals and the environment from the potential hazards of refrigerant gases.

Personal Protective Equipment

In the realm of HVACR safety, the selection and proper use of **personal protective equipment** (PPE) are paramount. Gloves and goggles serve as the first line of defense against direct contact with refrigerants and their potential hazards, such as frostbite and eye irritation. Gloves should be made of materials resistant to the chemicals in refrigerants, ensuring they do not degrade upon contact. Similarly, goggles should provide a seal around the eyes to prevent any accidental splashes from causing harm. These protective measures are not just recommendations but essential tools for safeguarding technicians against the immediate dangers presented by refrigerants.

In more extreme cases, where the risk of exposure is significantly higher, the use of a **self-contained breathing apparatus** (SCBA) may be necessary. SCBAs are critical in environments where refrigerant gases could displace oxygen, posing a risk of asphyxiation. This equipment allows technicians to work safely in confined spaces or in situations where a significant release of refrigerant gas is possible. The SCBA provides a breathable air supply, ensuring that technicians can perform their duties without the risk of oxygen deprivation. It's crucial that technicians are trained in the proper use and maintenance of SCBAs, as their effectiveness is contingent upon correct usage and regular inspection. The adherence to safety protocols, including the use of PPE, underscores the HVACR industry's commitment to the well-being of its professionals. By equipping technicians with the knowledge and tools necessary to mitigate exposure risks, the industry not only ensures the safety of its workforce but also promotes a culture of responsibility and professionalism.

Reusable Refrigerants

"rechargeable) cylinders for refrigerant recovery are essential tools in ensuring safety and compliance with environmental regulations. These cylinders are designed to be used multiple times, reducing waste and the need for disposable containers. It is crucial that technicians understand the proper handling, storage, and transportation of these cylinders to prevent accidents and ensure the integrity of the refrigerant for future use. **Proper labeling** is not just a regulatory requirement; it serves as a critical safety measure, providing immediate information about the contents, potential hazards, and necessary precautions. Additionally, technicians must be vigilant about **cylinder inspection** before each use to check for damage, corrosion, or compromised seals that could lead to leaks or contamination of the refrigerant. The use of **safety equipment**, such as gloves and goggles, cannot be overstated when handling refrigerants and their containers, regardless of whether they are deemed non-ozone depleting. This practice protects against frostbite, chemical burns, and inhalation of vapors that could lead to oxygen deprivation or other respiratory issues. Furthermore, understanding the **capacity limits** of rechargeable cylinders is vital to avoid overfilling, which can cause excessive pressure build-up and potentially result in cylinder failure or explosion. Adhering to the 80 percent fill rule, considering the ambient temperature and the specific refrigerant's density, is a guideline that ensures safety and compliance. Lastly, the **storage conditions** of these cylinders play a significant role in maintaining safety standards. Cylinders should be stored in a cool, dry, and well-ventilated area away from direct sunlight and sources of heat, which could increase internal pressure and risk of rupture. By following these guidelines, technicians can ensure the safe and effective recovery and recycling of refrigerants, contributing to environmental protection efforts and the sustainability of the HVACR industry."

Risks of Overfilling Cylinders

Overfilling refrigerant cylinders beyond the 80 percent capacity poses significant risks, primarily due to the expansion of refrigerants when exposed to increases in ambient temperature. This expansion can lead to dangerously high pressures inside the cylinder, risking a catastrophic failure of the cylinder itself. Such a failure not only poses immediate physical danger to anyone in the vicinity through the potential for explosion or rapid release of pressurized gas but also exposes individuals to the refrigerant's chemical hazards. Refrigerants can cause frostbite upon contact with skin or eyes due to their low boiling points when released into the atmosphere at normal pressures. Moreover, a rapid release of refrigerant gas can displace oxygen in the air, leading to possible asphyxiation risks for individuals in poorly ventilated spaces. The chemical exposure is particularly concerning with refrigerants that degrade into toxic compounds upon contact with open flames or hot surfaces, potentially producing phosgene gas, a toxic compound that can cause severe respiratory damage. Additionally, the environmental impact of releasing refrigerants into the atmosphere contributes to ozone depletion and global warming, contradicting the very regulations and safety protocols the EPA 608 certification aims to uphold.

Technicians must adhere to the 80 percent rule, accounting for the specific refrigerant's density and the ambient temperature conditions under which the cylinder will be stored or transported.

Nitrogen for Leak Detection

The choice of nitrogen over oxygen or compressed air for leak detection in HVACR systems is grounded in safety and efficiency. Nitrogen, an inert gas, does not support combustion, reducing the risk of fire or explosion that can occur when oxygen or compressed air comes into contact with oil residues or electrical components within the system. This characteristic makes nitrogen the preferred medium for pressurizing systems to test for leaks.

Using nitrogen for leak detection also avoids the introduction of moisture or oxygen into the system, which can lead to corrosion or oxidation of metal components, compromising the integrity and longevity of the system. Furthermore, nitrogen's dry and non-reactive nature ensures that it does not alter the chemical composition of the refrigerant or the oil in the system, maintaining the system's performance and reliability. The methodology for employing nitrogen in leak detection involves pressurizing the system with nitrogen to a specified pressure level and then monitoring the pressure gauge for any drop in pressure, which would indicate the presence of a leak. This method is highly effective in identifying even the smallest leaks, ensuring that they can be addressed before recharging the system with refrigerant. For technicians preparing for the EPA 608 certification, understanding the proper use of nitrogen in leak detection is crucial. It not only demonstrates compliance with safety standards but also reflects a commitment to best practices in HVACR system maintenance and repair. Mastery of this technique underscores the technician's capability to ensure system integrity, optimize performance, and uphold environmental standards by preventing the unnecessary release of refrigerants into the atmosphere.

Shipping

Refrigerant Cylinder Labeling Requirements

The **Department of Transportation (DOT) classification tag** is another critical label that must be affixed to refrigerant cylinders. This tag provides essential information regarding the transportation and handling regulations that apply to the cylinder, based on its contents. The DOT classification system categorizes chemicals and substances according to their risk factors, including flammability, corrosivity, and environmental hazards. For refrigerants, which can pose significant risks due to their pressure and chemical properties, the correct DOT classification ensures that they are transported in compliance with federal regulations, minimizing the risk of accidents or environmental damage. Each refrigerant cylinder must display a DOT classification tag that accurately reflects the specific refrigerant it contains. This tag informs handlers and transporters of the necessary precautions and legal requirements for shipping and handling the cylinder. For example, certain refrigerants may require special transportation conditions, such as temperature control or protection from direct sunlight, to prevent pressure build-up or degradation of the chemical. Furthermore, the DOT classification tag plays a crucial role in emergency response situations. In the event of an accident or leak, first responders can quickly identify the substance involved and implement the appropriate safety measures to protect themselves and the public.

Chapter 2: Type 1 Small Appliances

Recovery Requirements

Definition

Given the context of recovery requirements for Type 1 small appliances, it's essential to understand the specific procedures and protocols that must be followed to ensure compliance with EPA regulations and to safeguard environmental and personal safety. The recovery of refrigerants from small appliances, such as domestic refrigerators, window air conditioners, and dehumidifiers, involves critical steps to prevent the release of ozone-depleting substances into the atmosphere. The process includes the use of recovery equipment designed to extract refrigerant in either liquid or vapor form, ensuring that it is contained and not vented into the environment. This equipment must be EPA-certified and operated according to the manufacturer's instructions to achieve the required recovery efficiency levels.

Technicians must be adept at identifying the type of refrigerant in the appliance before beginning the recovery process, as mixing refrigerants can lead to equipment damage and reduce the purity of the recovered refrigerant, making it unsuitable for reuse or recycling. The importance of attaching the correct recovery cylinders, properly labeled for the specific refrigerant, cannot be overstressed. This not only prevents cross-contamination but also ensures that the refrigerant can be safely transported and stored until it can be recycled or properly disposed of. Furthermore, technicians must adhere to the evacuation requirements set forth for small appliances, which dictate the final vacuum pressure that must be achieved to consider the recovery process complete. These requirements vary depending on whether the appliance's compressor is operational and the date of manufacture of the recovery equipment used. Ensuring that these standards are met is crucial for minimizing the potential release of harmful refrigerants into the environment.

In addition to the technical aspects of refrigerant recovery, technicians must also prioritize safety by wearing appropriate personal protective equipment, such as gloves and goggles, to protect against potential exposure to refrigerants, which can cause frostbite or other injuries. The comprehensive understanding and application of these recovery requirements underscore the technician's role in environmental protection and compliance with federal regulations.

Evacuation for Small Appliances Pre-1993

For small appliances with and without working compressors, when utilizing recovery equipment manufactured before November 15, 1993, the evacuation requirements are distinct and tailored to ensure the safe and efficient removal of refrigerants. The guidelines set forth by the EPA mandate specific procedures to minimize the release of ozone-depleting substances during the recovery process. These procedures are critical for technicians to follow meticulously to comply with environmental regulations and to maintain the integrity of the refrigerant recovery and recycling system.

When dealing with small appliances that have non-operational compressors, the evacuation process must achieve a vacuum level sufficient to ensure that the majority of the refrigerant has been removed. For equipment manufactured before the specified date, the required vacuum level is less stringent, acknowledging the technological limitations of older recovery machines. However, technicians must still strive to reach the deepest vacuum possible with the equipment available, to reduce the potential for refrigerant release into the atmosphere. In the case of small appliances with working compressors, the evacuation requirements involve using the compressor to aid in the recovery of refrigerant. The process includes running the compressor to circulate the refrigerant towards the recovery equipment. Even with older recovery equipment, this method facilitates a more complete evacuation of refrigerant, leveraging the appliance's operational components to enhance the efficiency of the recovery process. Technicians must be aware of the type of refrigerant being recovered, as the evacuation requirements may vary slightly based on the refrigerant's properties. The use of recovery cylinders that are clearly labeled and designated for the specific type of refrigerant is essential to prevent cross-contamination and ensure the purity of the recovered refrigerant for recycling or proper disposal. Safety precautions during the evacuation process cannot be overstated. Technicians must employ personal protective equipment, including gloves and goggles, to safeguard against exposure to refrigerants, which can pose health risks. Additionally, ensuring that the recovery equipment is in good working condition and free from leaks is crucial to prevent accidental release of refrigerants during the evacuation process. The adherence to these evacuation requirements for small appliances, particularly when using older recovery equipment, underscores the technician's role in environmental stewardship. It reflects a commitment to upholding the highest standards of safety and efficiency in the handling of refrigerants. By following these guidelines, technicians contribute significantly to the efforts to protect the ozone layer and reduce the impact of climate change, aligning with the broader goals of the EPA 608 certification.

Evacuation for Small Appliances

For small appliances with and without working compressors, the evacuation requirements when utilizing recovery equipment manufactured after November 15, 1993, are more stringent and technologically advanced, reflecting the significant progress in refrigerant recovery technologies and methodologies. This evolution in equipment standards underscores the Environmental Protection Agency's commitment to enhancing environmental protection through more efficient and effective refrigerant recovery processes.

The post-1993 equipment is designed to achieve deeper vacuum levels, ensuring a more comprehensive evacuation of refrigerants and minimizing the potential for any residual refrigerants to escape into the atmosphere, which aligns with the overarching goal of reducing ozone depletion and global warming potential.

The specific evacuation requirements mandate that for small appliances, regardless of the compressor's operational status, the recovery equipment must be capable of evacuating the appliance to a level of 4 inches of mercury vacuum. Achieving this level of vacuum ensures that the majority of the refrigerant, whether in vapor or liquid form, is effectively removed from the appliance. This requirement is critical for preventing the release of refrigerants that contribute to ozone layer depletion and climate change. It is worth noting that the ability to reach and verify this vacuum level necessitates the use of recovery equipment equipped with accurate and reliable vacuum measurement tools, highlighting the importance of utilizing up-to-date and properly calibrated equipment. For technicians working on small appliances, it is imperative to understand and apply these evacuation standards diligently. This involves not only the technical capability to operate the recovery equipment effectively but also the procedural knowledge to ensure that all steps of the recovery process are conducted in compliance with EPA regulations. The process includes attaching the recovery equipment to the appliance, initiating the recovery process, monitoring the evacuation to achieve the required vacuum level, and then verifying that the vacuum level is maintained, indicating that the refrigerant has been adequately removed.

In addition to the technical and procedural aspects of refrigerant recovery, technicians must also prioritize environmental and safety considerations. This includes the proper handling and disposal of recovered refrigerants, ensuring that they are not released into the environment, and adhering to safety protocols to protect themselves and others from potential exposure to refrigerants. The use of personal protective equipment (PPE), such as gloves and goggles, is essential when handling refrigerants to prevent frostbite, inhalation, or other injuries. The post-1993 evacuation requirements for small appliances represent a critical component of the EPA's strategy to protect the environment and human health by reducing the release of harmful refrigerants. Technicians certified under EPA Section 608 play a vital role in this effort, and their adherence to these requirements is essential for ensuring the integrity of the refrigerant recovery and recycling system.

Recovery Techniques

Identifying Refrigerants and Noncondensables

The use of pressure and temperature measurements is a fundamental technique in the identification of refrigerants and the detection of noncondensable gases within refrigeration systems, especially when dealing with Type 1 small appliances. This method relies on the principle that each refrigerant has a specific pressure-temperature (P-T) relationship that is unique and can be used to accurately identify the type of refrigerant present in a system. By comparing the measured pressure and temperature values to the known P-T relationships of various refrigerants, technicians can determine the type of refrigerant in the system without the need for additional, potentially invasive testing methods.

To effectively utilize this technique, it is crucial for technicians to have access to accurate and up-to-date pressure-temperature charts or digital tools that provide this information for a wide range of refrigerants. The process begins with the technician measuring the pressure of the refrigerant within the system using a manifold gauge set. Following this, the temperature of the refrigerant is measured, typically at the same point where the pressure measurement was taken to ensure consistency and accuracy. These measurements must be precise, as even small deviations can lead to incorrect identification or the failure to detect noncondensable gases. Noncondensable gases, such as air, nitrogen, or other gases that do not condense at the operating temperatures of the refrigeration system, can significantly impact the efficiency and performance of the system. Their presence is often indicated by discrepancies between the measured P-T values and the expected values for the identified refrigerant. For instance, if the pressure of the system is higher than what would be expected for the measured temperature based on the refrigerant's P-T relationship, this discrepancy could suggest the presence of noncondensable gases.

Detecting noncondensable gases is critical, as their presence can lead to increased operating pressures, reduced cooling capacity, and can even cause damage to the system's components over time. Once identified, the removal of these gases is necessary to restore the system's efficiency and prevent further issues. This typically involves the evacuation of the refrigerant, followed by a vacuum process to remove the noncondensable gases, before recharging the system with the correct type and amount of refrigerant. In addition to identifying refrigerants and detecting noncondensable gases, the use of pressure and temperature measurements can also aid in diagnosing system issues and verifying proper system operation after maintenance or repair activities. For example, after recovering refrigerant from a small appliance and before recharging, technicians can use P-T measurements to ensure that the system is free of leaks and that the evacuation process has been completed successfully.

It is important for technicians to be thoroughly trained in the use of P-T charts and to understand the implications of the measurements they are taking. Misinterpretation of P-T data can lead to incorrect diagnoses, unnecessary component replacements, or the use of inappropriate refrigerants, all of which can have negative impacts on the system's performance and the environment. Therefore, ongoing education and practice in the use of pressure and temperature measurements are essential for all technicians working in the HVACR field, particularly those preparing for the EPA 608 certification exam. This knowledge not only supports compliance with environmental regulations but also enhances the technician's ability to provide high-quality, efficient service in the maintenance and repair of refrigeration systems.

Recovering Refrigerant from Small Appliances

Recovering refrigerant from small appliances with inoperative compressors necessitates a nuanced approach, given the inability to utilize the appliance's compressor to facilitate the recovery process. In such scenarios, a system-dependent recovery method, also known as a passive recovery method, is employed. This technique is particularly relevant for small appliances, such as domestic refrigerators, window air conditioners, and dehumidifiers, where the compressor is not functional, and the recovery of refrigerant must be conducted in a manner that ensures environmental protection and compliance with EPA regulations.

The essence of the system-dependent recovery method lies in its reliance on the pressure differential between the appliance and the recovery cylinder to transfer the refrigerant. To initiate this process, technicians must first ensure that the recovery cylinder is at a lower pressure than the refrigerant in the appliance. This can be achieved by cooling the recovery cylinder, often by placing it in a refrigerated environment or using ice, to lower its internal pressure. Once this condition is met, connecting the recovery cylinder to the appliance allows the refrigerant to flow naturally from the higher pressure zone within the appliance to the lower pressure zone within the cylinder.

It is imperative that technicians use EPA-certified recovery equipment even when employing system-dependent methods. The recovery equipment must be connected properly, with hoses attached to both the low-pressure and high-pressure sides of the appliance, if accessible. However, given the inoperative state of the compressor, the focus will predominantly be on accessing the refrigerant through the low-pressure side. The connection points must be secured tightly to prevent any potential leaks during the recovery process. Technicians must monitor the pressure within the recovery cylinder throughout the process, ensuring it does not exceed the cylinder's safe capacity. The **80 percent fill rule** must be adhered to, preventing overfilling and potential rupture of the recovery cylinder. This rule is not only a safety measure but also a regulatory requirement to mitigate the risk of accidental refrigerant release into the atmosphere.

Given the passive nature of system-dependent recovery methods, the process may be slower than active recovery methods that utilize the appliance's compressor. Technicians should be prepared for this and plan accordingly, especially when working in environments where multiple appliances require refrigerant recovery. Patience and attention to detail are crucial, as the complete evacuation of refrigerant from the appliance signifies not only adherence to environmental regulations but also the safeguarding of technician safety and the prevention of potential damage to the recovery equipment. Throughout the recovery process, the use of personal protective equipment (PPE) remains a critical consideration. Technicians must wear gloves and goggles to protect against accidental exposure to refrigerants, which can cause frostbite or other injuries due to their low temperatures. Additionally, technicians should work in well-ventilated areas to avoid inhalation of refrigerants or any decomposition products that may result from the recovery process.

In instances where the system-dependent method is not feasible or fails to recover all the refrigerant, technicians may need to resort to other approved recovery techniques. These may include the use of self-contained recovery equipment that can create a stronger vacuum to facilitate the removal of refrigerant. Regardless of the method employed, the ultimate goal remains the same: to recover refrigerants efficiently and safely, in compliance with EPA regulations, thereby contributing to the protection of the environment and the ozone layer. The meticulous application of system-dependent recovery methods for small appliances with inoperative compressors underscores the technician's role in environmental stewardship.

Installing Access Valves for Refrigerant Recovery

The installation of both high and low side access valves is a critical step in the refrigerant recovery process for small appliances with inoperative compressors. This procedure ensures that technicians can effectively manage the recovery process by providing access points for the recovery equipment to connect to the appliance's refrigeration system. The high side access valve is essential for connecting to the part of the system that operates under high pressure during normal operation, while the low side access valve connects to the part of the system that operates under lower pressure.

To properly install these valves, technicians must first identify the appropriate locations on the appliance's refrigeration system. The high side access valve is typically installed on or near the condenser or the liquid line, whereas the low side access valve is installed on or near the evaporator or the suction line. It is crucial that these valves are installed securely to prevent any potential leaks during the recovery process. The use of proper tools and adherence to safety protocols cannot be overstressed, as improper installation could not only lead to the release of refrigerants into the atmosphere but also pose risks to the technician. Once the access valves are installed, the technician can then connect the recovery equipment to these valves using appropriate hoses. The hoses must be capable of withstanding the pressures involved in the recovery process and should be checked for leaks before proceeding. The recovery equipment itself must be EPA-certified and capable of recovering refrigerant from both the high and low sides of the system. This dual capability is essential for ensuring that all refrigerant, whether in liquid or vapor form, can be effectively removed from the appliance.

The process of recovering refrigerant from small appliances with inoperative compressors through these installed access valves requires careful monitoring. Technicians must observe the pressure readings on the recovery equipment to ensure that the refrigerant is being evacuated efficiently and that the system is approaching the required vacuum level. This monitoring is critical for verifying that the recovery process is complete and that the appliance is free of refrigerant. In addition to the technical aspects of installing access valves and recovering refrigerant, technicians must also be mindful of the environmental implications of their work. The proper recovery of refrigerant not only complies with EPA regulations but also contributes to the global effort to reduce ozone depletion and climate change. Therefore, the meticulous execution of these procedures reflects the technician's commitment to environmental stewardship and professional responsibility.

The installation of both high and low side access valves, followed by the thorough and compliant recovery of refrigerant from small appliances with inoperative compressors, exemplifies the technical skill and environmental awareness required of HVACR technicians. This process, while specific in its requirements, underscores the broader principles of safety, efficiency, and environmental protection that are central to the HVACR industry.

Operating Compressors for Refrigerant Recovery

operating operative compressors during the refrigerant recovery process in Type 1 small appliances is a critical step that cannot be overlooked. This technique is particularly relevant when utilizing system-dependent recovery equipment, which relies on the compressor's functionality to facilitate the recovery of refrigerant. The compressor, in essence, acts as a pump, moving the refrigerant through the system and into the recovery unit. This method is not only efficient but also ensures that the maximum amount of refrigerant is recovered, minimizing the environmental impact and ensuring compliance with EPA regulations.

When recovering refrigerant from small appliances with operative compressors, it is essential to ensure that the compressor is in good working condition. Any malfunction could impede the recovery process or, worse, lead to the release of refrigerant into the atmosphere. Therefore, a preliminary check of the compressor's operational status is advisable before initiating the recovery process. This check should include an inspection for any signs of damage or wear that could affect its performance. Once the compressor's functionality is confirmed, the recovery process can commence. It is important to connect the recovery equipment correctly, ensuring that the high and low side access valves are properly attached. This setup facilitates the flow of refrigerant from the appliance to the recovery unit. The operation of the compressor will push the refrigerant out of the appliance and through the recovery machine, where it is collected in a recovery cylinder.

During the recovery process, monitoring the pressure gauges is crucial. These gauges provide real-time feedback on the system's pressure levels, indicating when the recovery process is complete. The goal is to reach a vacuum level as specified by the EPA, ensuring that almost all the refrigerant has been successfully removed from the appliance. It is also advisable to periodically check the recovery cylinder to avoid overfilling, adhering to the 80 percent fill rule to allow for the expansion of the refrigerant.

In addition to the operational aspects, safety precautions must be observed throughout the recovery process. Personal protective equipment, including gloves and goggles, should be worn to protect against potential exposure to refrigerant, which can cause frostbite or other injuries. Furthermore, ensuring a well-ventilated area for the recovery process is essential to mitigate the risk of refrigerant inhalation. The use of system-dependent recovery equipment in conjunction with operative compressors in small appliances is a technique that aligns with EPA guidelines and best practices in the HVACR industry. It not only ensures the efficient recovery of refrigerants but also underscores the importance of environmental stewardship and regulatory compliance.

Removing Solderless Access Fittings

Upon the completion of the refrigerant recovery process from small appliances, an essential step that must not be overlooked is the removal of solderless access fittings. These fittings are typically installed as a temporary measure to facilitate the recovery of refrigerant, especially in systems that were not originally equipped with service ports. While they serve an invaluable role during the recovery process, leaving them attached post-service poses significant risks.

The primary concern with leaving solderless access fittings in place is the potential for leaks. Even when tightly secured, these fittings are not as reliable as permanent, soldered connections. Over time, they may loosen due to vibration, temperature changes, or simply the degradation of sealing materials, leading to the escape of refrigerant into the atmosphere. This not only contravenes regulations aimed at preventing refrigerant emissions but also undermines the integrity of the appliance's refrigeration system.

Furthermore, the presence of unnecessary fittings on an appliance can create confusion during future maintenance or service activities. Technicians may mistakenly identify these temporary access points as official service ports, leading to incorrect diagnostic procedures or the introduction of contaminants into the system.

This can result in reduced efficiency, increased wear on components, or even system failure, necessitating costly repairs or replacements. To mitigate these risks, technicians must ensure that all solderless access fittings are removed once the recovery process is complete. This should be followed by properly sealing the system to maintain its integrity. If access to the system will be required for future servicing, consider installing permanent service valves by a qualified professional. This approach maintains the system's integrity and compliance with environmental regulations while facilitating future maintenance activities.

HFC-134a as Substitute for CFC-12

Hydrofluorocarbon (HFC)-134a, commonly referred to as R-134a, has emerged as a prominent substitute for chlorofluorocarbon (CFC)-12, or R-12, in the realm of Type 1 small appliances. This transition is pivotal in the context of environmental protection and regulatory compliance. R-134a is a single-component HFC refrigerant that possesses no ozone depletion potential (ODP), marking a significant advancement over its predecessor, R-12, which has been phased out due to its high ODP and global warming potential (GWP). The shift towards R-134a underscores the HVACR industry's commitment to adopting more eco-friendly refrigerants in line with international agreements such as the Montreal Protocol. The adoption of R-134a in small appliances, including domestic refrigerators, automotive air conditioning systems, and vending machines, is facilitated by its thermodynamic properties, which closely mimic those of R-12. This similarity allows for minimal modifications to existing systems when transitioning from R-12 to R-134a, although it is crucial to note that retrofitting involves more than merely substituting one refrigerant for another. Technicians must also consider the compatibility of lubricants, as R-134a typically requires polyester oils (POE) rather than the mineral oils commonly used with R-12. This compatibility is vital for the efficient operation of the refrigeration cycle and to prevent potential issues such as oil sludge formation which can impair system performance and longevity.

Furthermore, the transition to R-134a necessitates the use of specialized recovery and recycling equipment designed to handle HFCs. The Environmental Protection Agency (EPA) mandates the use of certified equipment to ensure the safe and effective recovery of R-134a, minimizing the risk of accidental release into the atmosphere. Technicians must be proficient in the use of such equipment and familiar with the procedures for safely handling and disposing of R-134a to comply with environmental regulations and safeguard against potential health hazards associated with refrigerant exposure.

In light of the evolving landscape of refrigerant use, the HVACR industry is witnessing a paradigm shift towards substances with lower environmental impact. R-134a serves as a bridge in this transition, offering a viable alternative to R-12 while the industry explores further innovations in refrigerant technology.

Safety

Refrigerant Decomposition at High Temps

Understanding the decomposition products of refrigerants at high temperatures is crucial for ensuring safety in handling and managing refrigerants, especially in the context of Type 1 small appliances. When refrigerants are exposed to high temperatures, either during equipment malfunctions, improper handling, or during processes such as welding and brazing near refrigerant lines, they can decompose and produce toxic and potentially harmful byproducts. These byproducts can pose significant health risks to technicians and anyone exposed, underscoring the importance of adhering to safety protocols and using personal protective equipment (PPE).

Chlorofluorocarbons (CFCs) and hydrochlorofluorocarbons (HCFCs), for instance, can decompose into substances such as hydrochloric acid (HCl) and hydrofluoric acid (HF) when subjected to high temperatures. These acids are highly corrosive and can cause severe burns upon contact with skin or mucous membranes. Additionally, the thermal decomposition of refrigerants can also release phosgene gas, a toxic compound that was used as a chemical weapon during World War I. Phosgene can cause severe respiratory distress and, in high concentrations, can be fatal. Hydrofluorocarbons (HFCs), while designed to be less harmful to the ozone layer and not containing chlorine, can still decompose under high temperatures and produce fluoride compounds, which are also harmful. The specific byproducts depend on the refrigerant's chemical composition and the conditions under which decomposition occurs, including the presence of catalysts, the temperature reached, and the duration of exposure to these conditions.

To mitigate the risks associated with the decomposition of refrigerants, technicians must follow best practices for safety, including:

- Avoiding the use of open flames or high-temperature devices near refrigerant lines whenever possible.
- Ensuring adequate ventilation in work areas to disperse any potentially harmful gases that may be released.
- Using PPE, such as gloves and goggles, to protect against exposure to corrosive substances. In situations where toxic gases may be released, the use of a self-contained breathing apparatus (SCBA) may be necessary to prevent inhalation of harmful byproducts.
- Adhering to proper refrigerant recovery, recycling, and disposal procedures to minimize the risk of accidental release or exposure to high temperatures.
- Undergoing continuous training and certification to stay informed about the latest safety protocols and refrigerant handling procedures.

The decomposition of refrigerants at high temperatures highlights the complex interplay between chemical safety and environmental protection. By understanding the potential hazards and implementing rigorous safety measures, technicians can protect themselves, the environment, and the public from the risks associated with refrigerant decomposition. This knowledge is not only a cornerstone of safe HVACR practices but also an essential component of professional responsibility in the field.

Chapter 3: Type 2 (High-Pressure)

Leak Detection

Leakage Signs in High-Pressure Systems

Excessive superheat and traces of oil around hermetic systems are indicative of potential leaks within high-pressure systems, which can significantly impact the efficiency and environmental safety of HVACR equipment. Excessive superheat refers to a condition where the refrigerant temperature is much higher than its saturation temperature at a given pressure, suggesting that the refrigerant is absorbing more heat than intended. This condition often arises from a low refrigerant charge due to a leak, causing the compressor to work harder and potentially leading to system failure. Technicians should carefully monitor superheat levels, as persistently high readings can pinpoint areas within the system where leaks may be occurring.

Traces of oil in hermetic systems serve as another critical indicator of leaks. Refrigerant and oil circulate together within the refrigeration system, with the oil lubricating the compressor and other moving parts. When a leak occurs, refrigerant gas escapes, and oil may seep out of the same points, accumulating around fittings, joints, or cracks. The presence of oil residue in these areas strongly suggests a refrigerant leak. Regular inspections for oil traces can help identify leaks early, preventing significant refrigerant loss and environmental harm. Addressing leaks in high-pressure systems promptly is crucial for maintaining system performance, ensuring safety, and complying with environmental regulations. Technicians should employ a systematic approach to leak detection, starting with visual inspections for oil residue, followed by the use of electronic leak detectors, ultrasonic detectors, or fluorescent dye systems to accurately locate the leaks. Once identified, repairs should be conducted as per EPA guidelines, ensuring that the system is properly evacuated and recharged to its correct refrigerant capacity.

Furthermore, maintaining detailed records of leak detection, repair, and maintenance activities is essential for regulatory compliance and for developing a proactive maintenance schedule. This approach not only helps in extending the lifespan of the equipment but also contributes to environmental conservation efforts by minimizing the release of refrigerants with high global warming potential (GWP) into the atmosphere. Technicians must also stay informed about the latest technologies and methods in leak detection and repair, as advancements in this field continue to offer new tools and techniques for improving the accuracy and efficiency of leak management in high-pressure systems. Continuous education and training play a vital role in equipping professionals with the knowledge and skills needed to effectively address the challenges of leak detection and repair, ensuring the safe and sustainable operation of HVACR systems.

Leak Testing Before Charging Equipment

Ensuring the integrity of high-pressure systems before charging or recharging with refrigerant is paramount to both operational efficiency and environmental protection. Leak testing serves as a critical preventative measure against the release of refrigerants into the atmosphere, which can contribute to ozone depletion and global warming. The process of leak testing involves pressurizing the system with a gas, typically nitrogen, and using electronic detectors, ultrasonic detectors, or soap solution methods to identify any points of escape. This step is crucial not only to comply with environmental regulations but also to maintain system performance and prevent costly refrigerant losses.

For high-pressure systems, the choice of test gas and the method of detection must be carefully considered to ensure the accuracy and safety of the test. Nitrogen, being inert and non-flammable, is preferred for pressurizing the system without introducing additional risks. The use of trace gases, such as hydrogen or helium in combination with nitrogen, can enhance the sensitivity of electronic leak detectors, allowing for the identification of leaks that might not be detected through traditional means.

Once a leak is detected, it must be promptly repaired, and the system should be retested to confirm the integrity of the repair. This iterative process of testing, repairing, and retesting is essential to fully secure the system against leaks. It is also important to document the location and severity of leaks, repairs undertaken, and the results of subsequent leak tests to maintain a record of system integrity over time.

The importance of leak testing extends beyond the immediate operational concerns. It reflects a broader commitment to environmental stewardship and regulatory compliance. The phasedown of hydrochlorofluorocarbons (HCFCs) and the transition to refrigerants with lower global warming potentials (GWPs) underscore the need for diligent leak detection and repair practices. By preventing the escape of high-GWP refrigerants into the atmosphere, technicians play a direct role in mitigating climate change and protecting the ozone layer. In practice, the implementation of leak testing protocols requires a thorough understanding of the system's design, the properties of the refrigerant in use, and the operational characteristics of leak detection equipment. Technicians must be adept at interpreting the signs of potential leaks, such as excessive superheat, the presence of oil at connection points, or unexplained losses of refrigerant charge. They must also be familiar with the regulatory requirements governing leak detection, repair, and recordkeeping to ensure full compliance with environmental laws.

The integration of leak testing into the routine maintenance and servicing of high-pressure systems is not just a regulatory obligation but a best practice that enhances system reliability, efficiency, and safety. It is a proactive measure that aligns with the goals of sustainability and environmental protection, reflecting the HVACR industry's ongoing efforts to reduce its ecological footprint. Through diligent leak testing and repair, technicians contribute to the broader objectives of the Montreal Protocol and the Clean Air Act, demonstrating the industry's commitment to responsible environmental management.

Leak Test Gas Preference Order

The selection of leak test gases is a critical decision in the process of ensuring the integrity of high-pressure systems. Nitrogen, due to its inert nature, stands out as the preferred choice for initial pressurization and testing. Its non-reactive and non-flammable characteristics make it an ideal candidate for safely identifying leaks without the risk of chemical reactions or combustion. When nitrogen is used alone, it provides a baseline method for detecting leaks through pressure drop tests or by using ultrasonic leak detectors that can identify the sound of gas escaping from a system.

However, the addition of a trace quantity of hydrochlorofluorocarbon (HCFC)-22, also known as R-22, to nitrogen introduces a specialized approach that enhances the leak detection process. This combination leverages the chemical properties of R-22, which can be more easily detected by certain types of electronic leak detectors designed to sense refrigerants. The trace amount of R-22 in the mixture acts as a signal for the leak detector, making it possible to identify leaks with greater sensitivity and specificity than when using nitrogen alone. This method is particularly useful in complex systems where leaks may be small or hidden in areas that are difficult to access or inspect visually. The preference for using nitrogen alone or nitrogen with a trace of R-22 over pure refrigerants for leak testing is rooted in both safety and environmental considerations. Pure refrigerants, especially those with high global warming potentials (GWPs), pose a risk of environmental harm if released. By using nitrogen or a nitrogen-R-22 mixture, technicians can minimize the potential for accidental refrigerant release during the testing phase. Additionally, the safety risks associated with handling pure refrigerants, including their flammability or toxicity, are significantly reduced when these alternatives are employed.

It is essential for technicians to be skilled in the application of both nitrogen and nitrogen-R-22 mixtures for leak testing. Understanding the operational characteristics of leak detection equipment and the properties of the gases being used is crucial for accurately identifying leaks. Technicians must also be aware of the environmental regulations governing the use of refrigerants, including R-22, to ensure compliance during the leak detection process. Proper training and certification in these techniques are vital for maintaining the integrity of high-pressure systems while upholding environmental and safety standards.

The implementation of these leak testing methods demonstrates a comprehensive approach to system maintenance and environmental responsibility. By selecting the appropriate test gas and employing effective leak detection techniques, technicians can ensure system reliability, prevent refrigerant loss, and contribute to the global effort to reduce the impact of refrigerants on the environment. The choice of nitrogen, either alone or with a trace of R-22, reflects a balanced consideration of safety, efficiency, and environmental stewardship in the field of high-pressure system maintenance.

Leak Repair Requirements

Allowable Leak Rate for Refrigeration

The Environmental Protection Agency (EPA) has set forth specific regulations regarding the allowable leak rate for commercial and industrial process refrigeration systems. These standards are part of a broader effort to minimize the environmental impact of refrigerant leaks, which can contribute to ozone depletion and global warming. For refrigeration systems containing more than 50 pounds of refrigerant, the allowable annual leak rate is as follows: 10% of the total charge for comfort cooling systems, 20% for commercial refrigeration systems, and 30% for industrial process refrigeration systems. This threshold is designed to prompt timely repairs and maintenance, ensuring that systems are operating efficiently and with minimal environmental harm.

To comply with these regulations, operators of such refrigeration systems must conduct regular leak inspections and promptly repair any leaks detected. The frequency of these inspections depends on the amount of refrigerant within the system. Systems with more than 50 pounds but less than 500 pounds of refrigerant are required to be inspected at least annually. For systems containing 500 to 2,000 pounds of refrigerant, semiannual inspections are mandated. Systems with over 2,000 pounds of refrigerant require quarterly inspections. Upon detection of a leak that exceeds the allowable rate, the operator has 30 days to repair the leak and must verify the repair within 45 days through follow-up leak testing. This rigorous approach ensures that leaks are not only promptly addressed but also effectively remediated to prevent recurrence. Additionally, operators are required to maintain detailed records of all inspections, leak detection efforts, repairs, and verifications for a minimum of three years. These records play a crucial role in demonstrating compliance with EPA regulations and can be subject to review during EPA inspections.

The significance of adhering to the allowable leak rate extends beyond regulatory compliance. By maintaining systems within the specified leak rate, operators can achieve greater operational efficiency, reduce costs associated with refrigerant loss and replenishment, and contribute to environmental sustainability. The reduction of refrigerant leaks is a critical component of the HVACR industry's efforts to mitigate its impact on climate change and ozone depletion. Technicians working on these systems must be thoroughly trained in leak detection techniques, repair procedures, and the proper handling of refrigerants. They must also be familiar with the types of refrigerants used in their systems and the specific environmental and safety risks associated with each. The transition to refrigerants with lower global warming potentials (GWPs) and ozone depletion potentials (ODPs) further underscores the need for specialized knowledge and skills in managing refrigeration systems.

The EPA's regulations on allowable leak rates are a key element of the broader regulatory framework governing the use and management of refrigerants. By enforcing these standards, the EPA aims to protect the environment while ensuring that refrigeration systems are used responsibly and sustainably. Operators and technicians alike play a vital role in achieving these objectives, underscoring the importance of education, certification, and ongoing professional development in the HVACR industry.

Allowable Leak Rate for Large Appliances

For appliances other than commercial refrigeration and industrial process refrigeration systems, which contain more than 50 pounds of refrigerant, the Environmental Protection Agency (EPA) has established different criteria for allowable leak rates. These appliances, which play a crucial role in various sectors, including HVAC systems in residential and commercial buildings, are subject to stringent regulations aimed at minimizing the environmental impact of refrigerant leaks. The allowable leak rate for these appliances is set at 20 percent of the total charge per year. This threshold is critical for ensuring that leaks are addressed promptly, thereby reducing the potential for environmental harm and maintaining the efficiency and reliability of the appliance.

The process for managing leaks in these appliances involves regular inspections, timely repairs, and accurate record-keeping. Operators of systems containing more than 50 pounds of refrigerant are required to conduct periodic leak inspections, with the frequency of these inspections determined by the amount of refrigerant within the system. Systems that fall into this category but do not meet the thresholds for commercial refrigeration or industrial process refrigeration must adhere to an inspection schedule that ensures compliance with the 20 percent leak rate standard. Upon the detection of a leak that exceeds the allowable rate, operators are mandated to repair the leak within 30 days and verify the effectiveness of the repair within 45 days through subsequent leak testing. This ensures that the repair has been successful in eliminating the leak and that the system is no longer at risk of exceeding the allowable leak rate. Operators must maintain comprehensive records of all leak detection activities, repairs, and verification tests for a minimum of three years. These records are essential for demonstrating compliance with EPA regulations and may be reviewed during inspections to ensure that the operator is adhering to the required standards.

The emphasis on reducing the allowable leak rate for appliances containing more than 50 pounds of refrigerant underscores the importance of proactive leak management practices. By identifying and repairing leaks early, operators can prevent significant refrigerant loss, which not only has environmental implications but also impacts the operational efficiency and cost-effectiveness of the appliance. The reduction of refrigerant leaks is a key component of efforts to mitigate climate change and protect the ozone layer, reflecting the HVACR industry's commitment to environmental stewardship. Technicians responsible for servicing these appliances must possess a deep understanding of leak detection techniques, repair methodologies, and the handling of various refrigerants. They must be equipped with the knowledge and tools necessary to effectively manage refrigerant leaks, ensuring that appliances are maintained within the allowable leak rate. The transition to refrigerants with lower global warming potentials and ozone depletion potentials further highlights the need for specialized skills and knowledge in managing these systems.

The EPA's regulations on allowable leak rates for appliances containing more than 50 pounds of refrigerant are a critical aspect of the broader effort to reduce the environmental impact of refrigerants. Through diligent compliance with these regulations, operators and technicians play a vital role in protecting the environment while ensuring the efficient and sustainable use of refrigeration systems.

Leak Repair Recordkeeping

Maintaining meticulous records of leak repairs is not merely a procedural requirement but a critical component of environmental stewardship and regulatory compliance within the HVACR industry. The Environmental Protection Agency (EPA) mandates that operators and technicians keep comprehensive documentation of all activities related to the detection, repair, and verification of leaks in high-pressure systems. This documentation serves multiple purposes: it provides a verifiable trail of compliance with federal regulations, aids in the diagnosis and prevention of future leaks, and contributes to the overall efficiency and longevity of the refrigeration system.

The recordkeeping process for leak repairs should include detailed information about the date of the leak detection, the methods used for detection, the specific location of the leak within the system, and the type and amount of refrigerant involved. Additionally, records must document the repair process in detail, including the date of repair, the techniques used to fix the leak, and the parts replaced or repaired. Following the repair, the system must be retested to ensure the leak has been effectively sealed. The results of this verification test, along with the date and method of testing, should also be included in the records. Operators are required to maintain these records for a minimum of three years, ensuring they are readily available for inspection by EPA officials upon request. This duration reflects the EPA's commitment to long-term environmental protection and system integrity. The records must be organized and stored in a manner that allows for easy retrieval and review, facilitating audits and compliance checks by regulatory bodies. The significance of accurate and thorough recordkeeping extends beyond regulatory adherence. It plays a vital role in the operational management of refrigeration systems. By analyzing historical data on leaks and repairs, technicians can identify patterns or recurring issues within the system, enabling proactive measures to prevent future leaks. This analytical approach can lead to improvements in system design, maintenance routines, and the selection of refrigerants and components, ultimately enhancing system performance and reducing environmental impact.

Furthermore, comprehensive leak repair records contribute to the industry's broader environmental goals. By documenting the successful repair of leaks and the prevention of refrigerant emissions, the HVACR industry can demonstrate its commitment to reducing its carbon footprint and protecting the ozone layer. This commitment is in line with the objectives of the Montreal Protocol and the Clean Air Act, which aim to phase out ozone-depleting substances and mitigate climate change. In the context of professional development and career advancement, the ability to effectively manage and document leak repairs is a valuable skill for technicians. It reflects a technician's proficiency in both the technical aspects of refrigeration systems and the regulatory environment in which they operate. As the industry continues to evolve, with increasing emphasis on sustainability and efficiency, technicians who excel in these areas are likely to find greater job stability, career progression opportunities, and recognition within the field.

The practice of diligent leak repair recordkeeping is a testament to the HVACR industry's dedication to environmental responsibility, regulatory compliance, and operational excellence. It underscores the critical role that technicians play in achieving these objectives, highlighting the importance of continuous education, certification, and adherence to best practices.

Recovery Techniques

Speeding Up Recovery Process

Recovering liquid refrigerant at the beginning of the recovery process significantly accelerates the overall procedure, a critical insight for technicians working with high-pressure systems. This technique leverages the physical properties of refrigerants, where liquid refrigerant is denser and can be removed more quickly than its vapor counterpart. By focusing on liquid recovery first, technicians can ensure a more efficient use of time and resources, minimizing the system's downtime and expediting service or repair tasks.

The process begins by attaching the recovery machine to the system's liquid line service valve. It's essential to ensure that the recovery tank is properly cooled, as this facilitates a faster transfer of refrigerant by maintaining a high pressure diffcrential between the system and the recovery tank. Cooling the recovery tank can be achieved through simple methods such as placing it in a shaded area or using a wet towel to wrap around the tank. This practice not only speeds up the recovery process but also helps in preventing the recovery machine from overheating.

Once the bulk of the liquid refrigerant has been recovered, the focus shifts to the vapor phase. It's crucial to understand that while recovering liquid refrigerant is faster, removing all the vapor is necessary to achieve a complete and thorough recovery. This step is vital for preventing any potential environmental harm and ensuring compliance with regulations that prohibit the release of refrigerants into the atmosphere. Technicians must monitor the recovery process closely, paying attention to the system's pressure gauges and the recovery machine's indicators. As the pressure in the system drops, the recovery speed will decrease, signaling that most of the liquid refrigerant has been removed. At this point, adjustments may be needed to optimize the recovery of the remaining vapor. In addition to the environmental and regulatory benefits, mastering the technique of prioritizing liquid refrigerant recovery offers practical advantages for technicians. It can lead to a reduction in the wear and tear on recovery equipment, as operating times are minimized, and the risk of overheating is reduced. Furthermore, this approach aligns with the industry's best practices, emphasizing efficiency, safety, and environmental responsibility. Technicians should also be aware of the specific characteristics of the refrigerants they are working with, as different refrigerants may require slight adjustments in the recovery process. However, the principle of prioritizing liquid recovery remains a constant best practice across different types of refrigerants and systems. Incorporating this technique into routine recovery operations not only enhances a technician's skill set but also contributes to their professional development. It demonstrates a commitment to excellence in service, adherence to environmental standards, and a proactive approach to safety and efficiency.

Speeding Recovery Methods

Heating the appliance or vessel from which refrigerant is being recovered presents another effective strategy for expediting the recovery process. This method takes advantage of the thermodynamic properties of refrigerants, where increasing the temperature of the substance decreases its density, causing it to vaporize more readily. By applying controlled heat to the exterior of the appliance or the vessel containing the refrigerant, technicians can significantly reduce the viscosity of the liquid refrigerant, facilitating a faster transition to its gaseous state and thereby speeding up the recovery process.

The application of heat can be achieved through various means, including the use of heat lamps, electric blankets, or even warm water baths, depending on the specific circumstances and the equipment available. It is crucial, however, to monitor the temperature closely to avoid overheating, which could potentially damage the appliance or alter the chemical stability of the refrigerant. The goal is to achieve a moderate increase in temperature that will expedite the vaporization of the refrigerant without compromising safety or equipment integrity. Furthermore, the technique of chilling the recovery vessel complements the heating of the appliance by creating a favorable pressure gradient that encourages the flow of refrigerant from the appliance into the recovery tank. The combined effect of heating the source and cooling the destination for the refrigerant maximizes the efficiency of the recovery process, reducing the time required to evacuate the system and minimizing the risk of environmental release.

Technicians employing these methods must be well-versed in the physical and chemical properties of the refrigerants they are working with, as well as the operational limits of the recovery equipment. Proper training and adherence to safety protocols are paramount, as is a thorough understanding of the environmental regulations governing the handling of refrigerants. By mastering these techniques, technicians can not only perform their duties more efficiently but also contribute to the broader goals of environmental protection and regulatory compliance.

The integration of these advanced recovery techniques into standard practice requires a commitment to ongoing education and professional development within the HVACR industry. As technologies evolve and new refrigerants are introduced, technicians must stay informed of the latest methods and tools available to them. This commitment to excellence and continuous improvement is essential for meeting the challenges of modern refrigeration and air conditioning systems, ensuring the health and safety of technicians and the communities they serve, and protecting the global environment for future generations.

Reducing Contamination with New Refrigerants

Reducing cross-contamination and emissions during the use of recovery or recycling machines with new refrigerants is a critical aspect of maintaining system integrity and environmental compliance. Cross-contamination not only degrades the performance of the refrigerant but also poses significant risks to the environment by releasing mixed refrigerants that are difficult to reclaim. To mitigate these risks, several strategies can be employed, focusing on equipment handling, refrigerant management, and technician training. Firstly, the use of dedicated recovery and recycling equipment for specific refrigerant types is highly recommended. This approach minimizes the risk of cross-contamination by ensuring that equipment is not shared between different refrigerant types. In situations where dedicated equipment is not feasible, thorough flushing of the recovery and recycling machines between uses is imperative. Flushing helps remove residual refrigerant and oil from the equipment, reducing the risk of contaminating the next batch of refrigerant to be recovered or recycled. The choice of flushing agent should be compatible with both the equipment and the refrigerants to avoid any chemical reactions that could damage the machinery or compromise the purity of the recovered refrigerant. Another key method involves the implementation of proper refrigerant identification practices before recovery or recycling. Technicians should use refrigerant identifiers to confirm the type of refrigerant in the system before beginning the recovery process. This step is crucial for preventing the unintentional mixing of refrigerants, which can occur if a system has been improperly serviced in the past. Accurate identification ensures that the correct recovery procedures are followed and that the refrigerant is handled appropriately throughout the recovery or recycling process.

Technicians must also adhere to best practices for refrigerant management, including the use of accurate, calibrated recovery equipment. Calibration ensures that the recovery machine operates within its specified parameters, efficiently separating refrigerant from contaminants such as oil and moisture. Additionally, maintaining optimal operating conditions for the recovery equipment, such as proper temperature and pressure settings, enhances the efficiency of the recovery process and reduces the likelihood of refrigerant emissions. Proper training and certification of technicians play a pivotal role in reducing cross-contamination and emissions. Technicians should be well-versed in the latest recovery and recycling techniques, as well as the environmental regulations governing refrigerant handling. Ongoing education and training ensure that technicians are equipped with the knowledge and skills necessary to adapt to new refrigerants and technologies, further minimizing the risk of cross-contamination and emissions. Finally, meticulous record-keeping and documentation of the refrigerant recovery and recycling process are essential. Detailed records help track the purity of recovered refrigerants and identify any instances of cross-contamination. This information is valuable for ensuring compliance with environmental regulations and for making informed decisions about the reuse or disposal of recovered refrigerants. By implementing these methods, technicians can significantly reduce the risks of cross-contamination and emissions when using recovery or recycling machines with new refrigerants. These practices not only protect the environment but also ensure the longevity and efficiency of HVACR systems, aligning with the industry's commitment to sustainability and regulatory compliance.

Checking System Pressure Stability

After achieving the required recovery vacuum, it is imperative to pause and observe the system's pressure for a few minutes. This waiting period is crucial as it allows any residual liquid refrigerant, which may still be present within the system or absorbed in the oil, to vaporize and reveal itself through a rise in system pressure. This phenomenon is a key indicator that not all refrigerant has been successfully recovered, necessitating further action. The presence of liquid refrigerant in the oil or elsewhere in the system can significantly impact the efficiency and environmental compliance of the recovery process. It is essential to ensure that all refrigerant, both in liquid and vapor forms, is completely removed from the system to prevent any potential release into the atmosphere, which would be in violation of environmental regulations and could harm the ozone layer. Technicians must be equipped with the knowledge and tools to accurately monitor system pressure and interpret the results. Utilizing precise and reliable pressure gauges is fundamental in this process. Should the system pressure begin to rise after reaching the recovery vacuum, this signals that additional recovery steps are necessary. The technician must then re-engage the recovery machine to remove the remaining refrigerant until the system pressure stabilizes at the desired vacuum level without subsequent increases. This meticulous approach ensures the thorough removal of refrigerants, aligning with both environmental standards and the technical requirements for system maintenance and repair. Understanding the properties of the refrigerant and the characteristics of the HVAC system in question is essential for technicians to effectively manage the recovery process. Different refrigerants and systems may exhibit unique behaviors under vacuum conditions, and familiarity with these nuances allows for more efficient and compliant recovery operations. For instance, some refrigerants may have a higher affinity for oil, requiring more time and specific techniques to fully extract from the system. The importance of this waiting period and subsequent actions cannot be overstated. It not only demonstrates adherence to environmental regulations but also reflects a technician's commitment to quality and safety in HVAC system servicing. By ensuring that all refrigerant is properly recovered, technicians prevent the potential for system contamination, maintain the integrity of the HVAC system, and contribute to the global effort to protect the environment from the harmful effects of refrigerant emissions. In addition to environmental and regulatory considerations, the complete recovery of refrigerants is also a matter of economic and operational efficiency. Residual refrigerants left in the system can complicate future maintenance and repair activities, potentially leading to increased costs and downtime for the system. Therefore, the practice of waiting to check for pressure increases after reaching the recovery vacuum serves multiple purposes, all of which contribute to the overall effectiveness and sustainability of HVAC system management.

Technicians must remain vigilant and patient during the recovery process, recognizing that the time invested in ensuring a complete recovery pays dividends in system performance, environmental protection, and regulatory compliance. This level of diligence is what distinguishes proficient technicians in the field of HVACR, underscoring the importance of thorough training and adherence to best practices in refrigerant recovery.

Recovery Requirements

Evacuation for High-Pressure Appliance Disposal

The evacuation of refrigerants from high-pressure appliances prior to disposal is a critical step that ensures environmental safety and compliance with federal regulations. The Environmental Protection Agency (EPA) mandates that all refrigerants be properly evacuated from HVACR equipment to prevent the release of substances that can deplete the ozone layer or contribute to global warming. For high-pressure appliances, the process of evacuation is particularly stringent due to the high pressures under which these systems operate and the potential for refrigerants, such as HCFCs and HFCs, to cause environmental harm if released.

When disposing of high-pressure appliances, technicians must adhere to specific evacuation levels to minimize the risk of refrigerant release into the atmosphere. The required evacuation level for appliances containing more than 15 pounds of refrigerant is to a level of 0 inches of mercury (inHg) vacuum, measured using a vacuum pump and an accurate vacuum gauge. This level ensures that virtually all the refrigerant has been removed from the system, significantly reducing the potential for any residual refrigerant to escape into the environment upon disposal.

The process involves connecting a recovery machine to the appliance and using the machine to draw down the pressure within the system. It is essential that the recovery machine used is certified for the type of refrigerant being recovered and is capable of achieving the required vacuum level. Technicians must monitor the evacuation process closely, ensuring that the system maintains the target vacuum level for a sufficient period to confirm that all refrigerant has been evacuated. This may involve multiple cycles of the recovery machine to fully evacuate the system, especially in cases where the appliance has a large refrigerant charge or complex piping that may trap refrigerant. Technicians must also be aware of the condition of the appliance being disposed of. If the appliance is damaged or has been exposed to conditions that could compromise the integrity of the refrigerant circuit, additional precautions may be necessary to ensure safe and complete evacuation. In some cases, accessing all parts of the system to ensure complete evacuation may require disassembly or additional steps to ensure that no refrigerant remains trapped within the appliance.

Upon completion of the evacuation process, the recovered refrigerant must be handled according to EPA regulations. This includes proper storage in DOT-approved cylinders, accurate labeling, and ensuring that the refrigerant is sent to a certified reclaimer if it cannot be reused. Documentation of the evacuation process, including the amount of refrigerant recovered and the final vacuum level achieved, is also a critical component of regulatory compliance. This documentation serves as proof of proper disposal and may be required for auditing purposes or to verify compliance with state and federal regulations. For technicians working in the field, understanding and adhering to the evacuation requirements for high-pressure appliance disposal is not only a matter of regulatory compliance but also an ethical responsibility to protect the environment. The proper evacuation of refrigerants is a key step in preventing their release into the atmosphere, where they can contribute to ozone depletion and climate change. As such, technicians play a crucial role in environmental stewardship, ensuring that the disposal of high-pressure appliances is conducted in a manner that minimizes environmental impact.

The EPA provides resources and training materials to support technicians in meeting these requirements, emphasizing the importance of proper refrigerant management in the HVACR industry. By following the established guidelines for refrigerant evacuation, technicians can ensure that they are part of the solution to environmental challenges, contributing to the sustainability of the industry and the protection of the planet for future generations.

Evacuation for Major vs. Non-Major Repairs

The evacuation requirements for high-pressure appliances vary significantly depending on whether the service being performed is classified as a major or non-major repair. This distinction is crucial for HVACR technicians to understand, as it directly impacts the procedural steps required for compliant and environmentally responsible refrigerant recovery and system servicing. Major repairs typically involve the disassembly of any part of the sealed system, such as the replacement of compressors, condenser coils, or evaporator coils. These components are integral to the system's operation and their repair or replacement can significantly affect the system's refrigerant charge and pressure. In contrast, non-major repairs may include tasks that do not directly involve the manipulation of the refrigerant circuit, such as electrical repairs or the replacement of external components not directly involved in the refrigeration cycle.

For major repairs on high-pressure appliances, the Environmental Protection Agency (EPA) mandates that technicians evacuate the refrigerant to a certain level to minimize the potential release of ozone-depleting substances into the atmosphere. The specific evacuation level required can depend on the type of refrigerant used in the system and the appliance's design. Typically, the target is to achieve a vacuum level that ensures the removal of as much refrigerant as possible without compromising the integrity of the system. This process not only adheres to environmental protection standards but also prepares the system for safe and effective repair or component replacement.

The evacuation process for major repairs involves several critical steps, starting with the proper identification and recovery of the refrigerant. Technicians must use recovery equipment that is certified for the type of refrigerant being handled and capable of achieving the required vacuum levels. The recovery machine should be connected to both the high and low sides of the system to efficiently remove the refrigerant. Monitoring the system's pressure with accurate gauges is essential to ensure that the evacuation reaches the desired vacuum level, which is often measured in inches of mercury (inHg) vacuum. In the context of non-major repairs, the evacuation requirements are generally less stringent. Since these repairs do not typically involve opening the refrigerant circuit, the focus is on ensuring that the system is not inadvertently vented during the service. However, technicians must still be prepared to recover any refrigerant that could be released and follow best practices for minimizing environmental impact. Non-major repairs require a thorough understanding of the system's operation to avoid unintentional damage or refrigerant loss. Even when the refrigerant circuit remains sealed, technicians should verify system pressure and check for leaks to ensure the integrity of the system before and after the repair is completed.

The distinction between major and non-major repairs underscores the importance of technician training and certification. Properly trained technicians can accurately assess the nature of the repair needed and apply the correct evacuation and recovery procedures. This not only ensures compliance with environmental regulations but also enhances the safety and reliability of the HVACR systems they service. As the industry continues to evolve with new refrigerants and technologies, the role of the technician in environmental stewardship and system efficiency becomes increasingly critical.

The adherence to EPA guidelines during the evacuation process is not only a legal requirement but also a measure of a technician's professionalism and commitment to environmental responsibility. For major repairs, once the target vacuum level is achieved, it is imperative to maintain this vacuum for a specified duration to verify that the system is indeed fully evacuated. This step, often referred to as a "standing vacuum test," helps to ensure that no hidden leaks are present and that the system can safely be opened for repairs or component replacement. The duration of this test can vary based on the appliance's size and complexity, but it is a critical component of the process that should not be overlooked. Technicians must also be aware of the potential for refrigerant release during the recharging of the system post-repair. The correct procedures for recharging involve careful measurement and handling of the refrigerant to avoid overcharging or introducing contaminants into the system. This is especially crucial after major repairs, as the system's characteristics may have changed, affecting its refrigerant capacity and operational pressures.

For non-major repairs, the emphasis remains on preventing any refrigerant release. Technicians should employ service practices that include the use of shut-off valves, proper hose connections, and leak detection equipment to ensure that the system remains sealed and intact throughout the repair process. Even though the refrigerant circuit is not directly involved, the potential for indirect effects on system pressure and integrity necessitates a cautious approach.

The differentiation between major and non-major repairs also highlights the need for detailed record-keeping. Documentation of the type of repair, the amount of refrigerant recovered or added, and the final system status is essential for compliance with EPA regulations. These records not only serve as evidence of proper procedure but also provide valuable information for future maintenance and service of the appliance. Technician certification plays a pivotal role in ensuring that these procedures are followed accurately. Certified technicians have demonstrated their knowledge and skills in handling refrigerants safely and are aware of the latest regulations and best practices. Their training includes not only the technical aspects of refrigerant recovery and system repair but also the environmental implications of their work. As such, certification is not just a professional credential; it is a testament to a technician's ability to contribute positively to environmental conservation efforts.

In the dynamic field of HVACR, continuous learning and adherence to best practices are essential for professional growth and environmental protection. The distinction between major and non-major repairs, and the corresponding evacuation requirements, exemplify the nuanced understanding required to service high-pressure appliances effectively. By following these guidelines, technicians not only ensure the operational efficiency and safety of the systems they work on but also uphold their responsibility towards environmental stewardship. This commitment to excellence and sustainability is what defines the modern HVACR professional, reflecting the industry's broader goals of innovation, efficiency, and environmental protection.

Evacuation for Leaky vs. Non-Leaky Appliances

When addressing the evacuation requirements for high-pressure appliances, it's crucial to differentiate between leaky and non-leaky systems. This distinction is not merely procedural but is rooted in the environmental and safety implications of handling refrigerants. For non-leaky appliances, the evacuation process is straightforward, aiming to ensure that the system is devoid of refrigerants before servicing or disposal. The primary goal is to minimize the potential release of harmful refrigerants into the atmosphere, adhering to the stringent regulations set forth by the Environmental Protection Agency (EPA).

The process begins with a thorough inspection of the appliance to confirm its integrity and to ensure that it is indeed non-leaky. This step is critical as it determines the subsequent procedures and safety precautions that need to be in place. Following this, technicians must employ recovery machines designed to handle the specific type of refrigerant used in the appliance. These machines are equipped with features that allow for the efficient and safe removal of refrigerants, ensuring that the process meets the regulatory requirements.

For leaky appliances, the evacuation requirements are more complex. The presence of leaks introduces additional risks, not only to the environment but also to the technician performing the recovery. Leaks can lead to the unintended release of refrigerants, which are often greenhouse gases with high global warming potential. Therefore, identifying and repairing leaks before the evacuation process is paramount. This not only aids in the conservation of the refrigerant but also ensures the safety of the technician and the environment. Technicians must use specialized equipment to detect leaks, which can range from simple visual inspections to the use of sophisticated electronic leak detectors. Once leaks are identified, they must be promptly repaired using techniques that ensure the long-term integrity of the appliance. Only after all leaks have been addressed can the evacuation process proceed. This approach underscores the importance of meticulous preparation and adherence to best practices in the handling of high-pressure appliances, especially those that are leaky.

The evacuation process for leaky appliances requires a heightened level of vigilance and expertise. Technicians must navigate the challenges posed by the compromised system, ensuring that all refrigerant is recovered without exacerbating the existing leaks. This often involves the use of more advanced recovery techniques and equipment, capable of precisely managing the removal of refrigerants from a leaky system. The goal remains the same: to safely and effectively evacuate the appliance of all refrigerants, thereby mitigating the environmental impact and ensuring compliance with EPA regulations.

The meticulous approach required for the evacuation of refrigerants from leaky high-pressure appliances underscores the critical nature of this process. It is not merely about removing the refrigerant but doing so in a manner that prevents any further harm to the environment or risk to human health. The use of advanced recovery techniques and equipment becomes indispensable in these scenarios. These tools are designed to ensure that even in the presence of leaks, the refrigerant is recovered efficiently, minimizing any potential for release into the atmosphere. The process involves careful monitoring of the recovery equipment to ensure that it operates within the specified parameters, effectively removing all traces of refrigerant from the system. In addition to the technical aspects of the evacuation process, there is a significant emphasis on the documentation and record-keeping associated with handling leaky appliances. Technicians are required to meticulously document the condition of the appliance, the nature and location of leaks, the amount of refrigerant recovered, and the repair methods employed to address the leaks. This documentation is not only a regulatory requirement but also serves as a critical record that contributes to the broader efforts of environmental protection and refrigerant management.

The distinction between leaky and non-leaky appliances also highlights the importance of ongoing education and training for technicians. Given the evolving nature of refrigerant regulations and the introduction of new technologies, technicians must stay informed about the latest best practices in refrigerant recovery and leak repair. This includes understanding the environmental implications of different types of refrigerants, the impact of leaks on global warming and ozone depletion, and the most effective strategies for leak detection and repair.

Ultimately, the evacuation requirements for high-pressure appliances, whether leaky or non-leaky, reflect a comprehensive approach to environmental stewardship and safety. By adhering to these requirements, technicians play a crucial role in protecting the atmosphere from the harmful effects of refrigerant emissions. The process is a testament to the industry's commitment to responsible refrigerant management, ensuring that appliances are serviced, repaired, and disposed of in a manner that prioritizes the health of the planet and its inhabitants. Through diligent adherence to these practices, the HVACR industry continues to make strides in reducing its environmental footprint, one appliance at a time.

Evacuation for High-Pressure Appliances

The evacuation requirements for high-pressure appliances, particularly when considering the appliance or component containing less versus more than 200 pounds of refrigerant, necessitate a detailed understanding of the procedures and regulations that govern such operations. The Environmental Protection Agency (EPA) mandates specific evacuation levels to ensure the safe and efficient removal of refrigerants, minimizing potential environmental harm. For appliances containing less than 200 pounds of refrigerant, the required evacuation level to achieve before the appliance can be opened for maintenance, service, or disposal is 10 inches of mercury vacuum. This standard aims to ensure that the majority of the refrigerant is recovered, thereby reducing the risk of release into the atmosphere.

Conversely, for appliances or components containing more than 200 pounds of refrigerant, the evacuation requirement is more stringent, necessitating an evacuation level down to 15 inches of mercury vacuum. This heightened requirement reflects the greater potential environmental impact due to the larger quantity of refrigerant. The deeper vacuum level ensures a more comprehensive removal of refrigerant, further mitigating the risk of any residual refrigerant escaping into the environment. It is crucial for technicians to utilize appropriate recovery equipment capable of achieving these specified vacuum levels, ensuring compliance with EPA regulations.

Technicians must also be aware of the type of refrigerant being recovered, as this can influence the approach and equipment used during the evacuation process. The use of recovery machines designed for the specific type of refrigerant ensures efficiency and compliance with environmental standards. Additionally, technicians should conduct a thorough inspection of the appliance or component prior to the evacuation process to identify any leaks or damage that could affect the recovery process. Addressing these issues beforehand ensures a smoother and more effective evacuation, aligning with the overarching goal of environmental protection and safety.

The distinction between appliances containing less than and more than 200 pounds of refrigerant underscores the tailored approach required to handle different volumes of refrigerant. This differentiation ensures that the evacuation process is appropriately scaled to the environmental risk posed by the refrigerant volume, with more rigorous standards applied to larger systems. It is imperative for technicians to adhere to these regulations, employing precision and care in their work to safeguard the environment and comply with legal requirements. Furthermore, the evacuation process is not solely about meeting regulatory benchmarks but also about ensuring the integrity and longevity of the HVACR systems. Proper evacuation prevents the potential contamination of refrigerant, which can compromise system performance and efficiency. Technicians must be diligent in following the prescribed evacuation procedures, utilizing their training and expertise to perform the task effectively. This not only fulfills regulatory obligations but also contributes to the responsible management and operation of HVACR systems, aligning with the industry's commitment to environmental stewardship and sustainability.

In the context of high-pressure appliances, the detailed attention to evacuation requirements based on refrigerant volume highlights the nuanced approach necessary to address environmental concerns. The EPA's regulations are designed to minimize the release of harmful refrigerants, reflecting a broader commitment to protecting the atmosphere and combating climate change. By adhering to these standards, technicians play a vital role in the responsible management of refrigerants, contributing to the health and safety of the environment.

This responsibility underscores the importance of comprehensive training and adherence to best practices in the field of HVACR, ensuring that technicians are well-equipped to meet the challenges of modern refrigerant management.

Evacuation for Pre/Post-1993 Equipment

The distinction between recovery/recycling equipment manufactured before versus after November 15, 1993, plays a pivotal role in the evacuation requirements for high-pressure appliances. This differentiation is not arbitrary but is deeply rooted in the technological advancements and regulatory changes that have occurred over time, impacting the efficiency and environmental safety of refrigerant recovery processes. Equipment manufactured before this date often lacks the enhancements and features that newer models incorporate, designed to meet or exceed the stringent standards set forth by the Environmental Protection Agency (EPA).

For high-pressure appliances, utilizing recovery/recycling equipment built before November 15, 1993, technicians may encounter limitations in the equipment's ability to achieve the desired vacuum levels efficiently. These older models may not be as effective in minimizing the release of refrigerants into the atmosphere, potentially compromising environmental safety and compliance with current regulations. Therefore, it is imperative for technicians to be acutely aware of the capabilities and limitations of the equipment they are using, ensuring that it is still capable of meeting the required evacuation standards mandated by the EPA. In some cases, additional steps or equipment may be necessary to supplement the evacuation process, ensuring that all refrigerant is adequately recovered and that the system is properly evacuated to the required levels. On the other hand, recovery/recycling equipment manufactured after November 15, 1993, is designed with modern technologies and features that align with the latest EPA regulations and standards. These newer models are more efficient at achieving the necessary vacuum levels for high-pressure appliances, ensuring a more thorough and environmentally safe recovery of refrigerants. They often incorporate advanced features such as automatic shut-off to prevent the release of refrigerants into the atmosphere, digital monitoring systems for precise control over the evacuation process, and improved compatibility with a wider range of refrigerants, including those with lower global warming potentials.

The use of equipment built after November 15, 1993, not only facilitates compliance with EPA regulations but also enhances the overall efficiency and effectiveness of the refrigerant recovery process. It represents a commitment to environmental stewardship and reflects the HVACR industry's ongoing efforts to adopt practices and technologies that reduce the environmental impact of refrigerant emissions. Technicians working with high-pressure appliances must ensure that their recovery/recycling equipment is up to date, capable of performing the required tasks to the highest standards, and in alignment with current environmental and safety regulations. Moreover, the transition to using equipment manufactured after November 15, 1993, underscores the importance of continuous education and training for technicians. Staying informed about the latest advancements in recovery/recycling technologies and understanding the operational differences between older and newer equipment models are crucial for ensuring effective refrigerant management. This knowledge not only aids in achieving regulatory compliance but also in promoting best practices within the industry, contributing to the overall goal of minimizing the HVACR sector's environmental footprint.

In the context of high-pressure appliances, the choice of recovery/recycling equipment—whether built before or after November 15, 1993—has significant implications for the evacuation process. It affects the efficiency of refrigerant recovery, the environmental impact of the process, and compliance with regulatory standards. As such, technicians must carefully consider the capabilities of their equipment, opting for newer models whenever possible to take advantage of technological advancements and to ensure adherence to the highest standards of environmental protection and safety. This approach not only benefits the technician and the industry but also contributes to the broader efforts to protect the environment from the potential harms associated with improper refrigerant management.

Prohibition on System-Dependent Equipment

The prohibition on using system-dependent recovery equipment on systems containing more than 15 pounds of refrigerant is a critical regulation that technicians must adhere to during the refrigerant recovery process. This mandate is rooted in the need to ensure that the recovery of refrigerants from larger systems is conducted in a manner that minimizes the risk of accidental release into the atmosphere, thereby protecting environmental and public health. System-dependent recovery equipment, often used for smaller appliances, lacks the capacity and efficiency required for handling the larger volumes of refrigerant found in high-pressure systems. These systems, due to their size and complexity, necessitate the use of more sophisticated recovery machines that are designed to manage and contain refrigerants effectively during the recovery process.

The rationale behind this prohibition is multifaceted, focusing on both environmental protection and the practical aspects of refrigerant recovery. Larger HVACR systems, which contain more than 15 pounds of refrigerant, are typically found in commercial and industrial settings. The volume of refrigerant in these systems, if released, could have a significant impact on the ozone layer and contribute to global warming. Therefore, the use of recovery equipment that is specifically designed for such volumes is essential.

These machines are equipped with features that allow for the efficient recovery of refrigerants, including the ability to handle both liquid and vapor phases, thereby ensuring that the maximum amount of refrigerant is recovered and properly recycled or disposed of. Moreover, the use of appropriate recovery equipment for high-pressure systems is also a matter of safety. The process of recovering refrigerant from these systems can be hazardous if not done correctly, with risks including exposure to refrigerants under pressure, which can cause frostbite or other injuries. Advanced recovery machines are built to mitigate these risks, providing features such as automatic shut-off valves, pressure gauges, and hoses designed to withstand high pressures, thereby ensuring the safety of technicians during the recovery process.

Compliance with this prohibition also reflects a technician's professionalism and commitment to industry best practices. It demonstrates an understanding of the importance of using the right tools for the job, which is a fundamental aspect of HVACR work. Technicians who adhere to this regulation contribute to the industry's reputation for safety, reliability, and environmental stewardship. This commitment is particularly important in an era where environmental concerns are increasingly at the forefront of public consciousness. By using the correct recovery equipment, technicians play a direct role in reducing the HVACR industry's environmental footprint, aligning with broader efforts to combat climate change and ozone depletion. The prohibition is enforced through various mechanisms, including certification requirements, which ensure that technicians have the necessary knowledge and skills to select and use recovery equipment appropriately.

The EPA's certification exam for HVACR technicians includes sections on refrigerant recovery, including questions designed to test a technician's understanding of the regulations governing the use of recovery equipment. This ensures that all certified technicians are aware of the prohibition and understand the reasons behind it. In addition to certification, the industry also relies on manufacturers and distributors to provide guidance on the selection and use of recovery equipment. Manufacturers typically provide detailed specifications for their equipment, including the maximum refrigerant capacity, making it easier for technicians to choose the right tools for each job. Distributors, meanwhile, play a key role in educating technicians about the latest recovery technologies and the regulatory requirements that govern their use.

The prohibition on using system-dependent recovery equipment for systems containing more than 15 pounds of refrigerant is a clear example of how regulations can drive improvements in industry practices, leading to better environmental outcomes and safer working conditions. By adhering to this regulation, technicians ensure that refrigerant recovery is conducted efficiently, safely, and in compliance with environmental standards, reflecting the HVACR industry's commitment to excellence and sustainability.

Refrigeration

Identifying Refrigerants in Appliances

Identifying refrigerants in appliances is a critical skill for HVACR technicians, requiring a comprehensive understanding of the various types of refrigerants and their applications in high-pressure systems. The process begins with recognizing the labeling on refrigerant cylinders and appliances, which is standardized to avoid confusion and ensure safety. Each refrigerant type, whether it be R-22, R-410A, or another, is designated by a unique color code on its cylinder. This visual cue is the first step in identification, providing a quick reference for technicians. However, reliance solely on color coding is insufficient due to the possibility of cylinder misuse or labeling errors. Therefore, further verification methods are necessary.

The next step involves consulting the appliance's nameplate, which contains vital information including the type of refrigerant it uses. This data is crucial, especially when servicing or repairing equipment, to ensure compatibility and efficiency. The nameplate also offers insights into the appliance's operational specifications, such as pressure ranges and electrical requirements, which are essential for proper maintenance and troubleshooting. For a more in-depth analysis, technicians may employ refrigerant identifiers, sophisticated tools designed to analyze the chemical composition of the refrigerant within a system. These devices provide accurate readings, helping to prevent the mixing of incompatible refrigerants, which can lead to system damage, reduced efficiency, or even safety hazards. The use of refrigerant identifiers is particularly important in systems where the refrigerant type is unknown or in cases where cross-contamination is suspected.

Another method involves the use of pressure-temperature (PT) charts, which display the relationship between the refrigerant's pressure and its temperature. By measuring the system's pressure and comparing it to the expected temperature on the PT chart, technicians can verify the refrigerant type. This method requires precise instruments and a thorough understanding of thermodynamic principles, as the readings must be interpreted in the context of the system's current operating conditions.

Technicians must also be aware of the legal and environmental implications of refrigerant handling. The Clean Air Act and the Environmental Protection Agency (EPA) regulations mandate specific procedures for the recovery, recycling, and disposal of refrigerants. Knowledge of these regulations is not only critical for compliance but also for the protection of the environment. The Montreal Protocol, an international treaty, further underscores the global commitment to phasing out ozone-depleting substances, including certain types of refrigerants. This highlights the importance of correct refrigerant identification and handling in the broader context of environmental stewardship. In addition to regulatory knowledge, technicians must possess practical skills in refrigerant recovery and recycling. This includes the use of recovery machines and the adherence to best practices for minimizing refrigerant loss and preventing contamination. The selection of appropriate recovery equipment, based on the type of refrigerant and the specifics of the appliance, is a key factor in the efficient and safe management of refrigerants.

The complexity of refrigerant identification and handling underscores the need for continuous education and training in the HVACR field. Technicians must stay abreast of technological advancements, regulatory changes, and the introduction of new refrigerants to the market. This ongoing learning process is essential for maintaining the highest standards of professionalism and ensuring the effective operation of high-pressure appliances. Furthermore, the role of manufacturers and industry organizations in providing accurate and up-to-date information cannot be overstated. Access to reliable resources, including technical manuals, online databases, and training programs, is invaluable for technicians seeking to enhance their skills and knowledge. Collaboration within the HVACR community, through forums and professional networks, also contributes to the collective understanding of refrigerant identification and management. In the context of high-pressure appliances, the ability to accurately identify refrigerants is more than a technical skill; it is a critical component of environmental responsibility, safety, and regulatory compliance. The methods and tools available to technicians, combined with a solid foundation in HVACR principles, enable the effective and responsible handling of refrigerants. This, in turn, supports the broader goals of environmental protection, system efficiency, and customer satisfaction, reinforcing the essential role of skilled technicians in the HVACR industry.

Pressure-Temperature of High-Pressure Refrigerants

Understanding the pressure-temperature relationships of common high-pressure refrigerants is crucial for HVACR technicians. This knowledge not only aids in the proper identification of refrigerants but also in the diagnosis and troubleshooting of refrigeration systems. The pressure-temperature (P-T) chart is an essential tool in this regard, providing a direct correlation between the pressure of the refrigerant within the system and its temperature.

For high-pressure refrigerants, such as R-410A, R-22, and R-134a, the P-T chart details specific temperatures at various pressures, measured in pounds per square inch gauge (psig). It's important to note that the psig readings on your gauges must be converted to pounds per square inch absolute (psia) by adding 14.7, which is the atmospheric pressure at sea level. This conversion is critical for accurate readings and interpretations of the refrigerant's behavior under different conditions. For instance, R-410A, a common high-pressure refrigerant used in many modern HVAC systems, exhibits a specific pressure at room temperature (approximately 75°F) that significantly differs from R-22, a refrigerant phased out due to its ozone-depleting potential but still present in older systems. Understanding these differences is vital for effective system diagnosis and maintenance.

When working with these refrigerants, technicians must be adept at using the P-T chart to determine if a system is properly charged, identify potential leaks, or diagnose issues related to compressor performance. For example, if the measured pressure of an R-410A system at a given temperature is lower than what is indicated on the P-T chart, it may suggest a refrigerant leak or an undercharged system. Conversely, higher-than-expected pressures could indicate an overcharged system or potential blockages in the refrigerant circuit.

Moreover, the P-T chart is indispensable when charging a system. By knowing the ambient temperature and referring to the chart, technicians can accurately gauge the amount of refrigerant needed for optimal performance. This precision ensures the system operates efficiently, reducing energy consumption and wear on components. In addition to the practical applications, the P-T chart also underscores the importance of safety. High-pressure refrigerants, by their nature, can pose risks if not handled correctly. Knowledge of the pressure-temperature relationship helps technicians take appropriate precautions, such as using the correct recovery equipment and wearing personal protective gear, to mitigate these risks.

Lastly, the evolving landscape of refrigerants, driven by environmental regulations and technological advancements, makes the understanding of pressure-temperature relationships even more critical. As new refrigerants are introduced to replace older, high-global warming potential (GWP) substances, technicians must stay informed about their properties, including pressure-temperature characteristics, to ensure safe and effective HVACR system servicing. In essence, the mastery of pressure-temperature relationships, facilitated by the P-T chart, is foundational for HVACR technicians. It enables precise system diagnostics, efficient refrigerant charging, and adherence to safety standards, all of which contribute to the optimal performance of high-pressure refrigeration systems and the advancement of environmental and professional goals within the HVACR industry.

High-Pressure Appliance Components

Understanding the components of high-pressure appliances and the state of refrigerant within them is essential for HVACR technicians to ensure the efficient and safe operation of these systems. High-pressure appliances, such as air conditioners and heat pumps that use refrigerants like R-410A, R-22, or R-134a, have several key components, each playing a critical role in the refrigeration cycle. These components include the receiver, evaporator, accumulator, compressor, and condenser, among others. The state of the refrigerant—whether vapor or liquid—varies throughout the system, influenced by the function of each component.

The receiver is a storage tank for the refrigerant and is located after the condenser in the refrigeration cycle. It holds the liquid refrigerant that exits the condenser and ensures a steady supply to the expansion valve. The refrigerant within the receiver is in a liquid state, under high pressure, which is crucial for the controlled release of refrigerant into the evaporator. The evaporator plays a pivotal role in absorbing heat from the environment, such as indoor air in the case of air conditioning systems. As the liquid refrigerant enters the evaporator, it evaporates, changing from a liquid to a vapor.

This phase change allows the refrigerant to absorb heat, cooling the surrounding area. The refrigerant in the evaporator is primarily in a vapor state, although it begins as a liquid at the inlet. The accumulator is located between the evaporator and the compressor and serves to protect the compressor from liquid refrigerant damage. It collects any residual liquid refrigerant that did not evaporate in the evaporator, preventing it from entering the compressor. The refrigerant in the accumulator is a mixture of vapor and liquid, with the design ensuring that only vapor enters the compressor.

The compressor is the heart of the refrigeration cycle, responsible for circulating refrigerant throughout the system. It compresses the refrigerant vapor from the evaporator, raising its pressure and temperature, and then pushes it towards the condenser. The refrigerant in the compressor is in a vapor state, as compressing liquid refrigerant could cause damage to the compressor. The condenser is where the refrigerant vapor releases the absorbed heat to the outside environment, condensing back into a liquid state. This component is crucial for the continuous cycle of refrigeration, allowing the refrigerant to expel heat and then return to the evaporator to absorb more. The refrigerant enters the condenser as a high-pressure vapor and exits as a high-pressure liquid, ready to be stored in the receiver or directed back into the cycle.

Each of these components is designed to handle refrigerant in specific states—vapor or liquid—under varying pressures. The precise control of refrigerant state and pressure is what makes modern refrigeration and air conditioning possible. Technicians must thoroughly understand these components and the refrigerant states within them to diagnose, maintain, and repair high-pressure refrigeration systems effectively.

Safety

Energizing Compressors Under Vacuum

Energizing hermetic compressors under vacuum conditions can lead to severe damage to the compressor's internal mechanisms. This practice is highly discouraged due to the potential for causing immediate and irreversible harm to the compressor unit. When a hermetic compressor is energized under vacuum, the lack of sufficient refrigerant mass flow through the compressor can result in inadequate cooling and lubrication of the compressor's moving parts. This scenario increases the risk of overheating, which can lead to the breakdown of the compressor's motor winding insulation and other critical components.

The absence of refrigerant flow under vacuum conditions means that the compressor's motor relies solely on the refrigerant for cooling. Without this cooling effect, temperatures can rise rapidly, leading to thermal overload and eventual failure. Additionally, the lubrication within the system, which is designed to circulate with the refrigerant, will not adequately reach all necessary components, further increasing the risk of wear and damage.

To prevent such occurrences, it is essential to ensure that the system is not under vacuum before energizing the compressor. Technicians should verify that the system has been properly charged with refrigerant to a level that ensures both effective cooling and lubrication. This can be achieved by following proper evacuation and charging procedures, which include using a reliable vacuum pump to remove air and moisture from the system, followed by accurately charging the system with the correct type and amount of refrigerant as specified by the manufacturer. Moreover, implementing a series of checks before starting the compressor, such as verifying pressure levels with gauges and ensuring that all valves are in the correct position, can further safeguard against the risks associated with energizing under vacuum. These preventive measures not only protect the compressor and extend its lifespan but also uphold the safety standards and operational efficiency of the entire HVACR system. Adhering to these guidelines ensures that technicians maintain a high level of professionalism and competence in handling high-pressure refrigeration systems, ultimately contributing to their career growth and the advancement of industry standards.

ASHRAE Standard 15 Equipment Room Requirements

ASHRAE Standard 15 sets forth stringent requirements for equipment rooms housing refrigeration systems, emphasizing the need for oxygen deprivation sensors across all types of refrigerants. This mandate is in place to ensure the safety and well-being of personnel who may be exposed to environments where refrigerant leaks could lead to oxygen displacement, posing serious health risks. Oxygen deprivation sensors are critical in these settings, as they provide an early warning system that can alert staff to evacuate or take corrective action before oxygen levels drop to dangerous levels. The presence of these sensors is not just a recommendation but a requirement under ASHRAE Standard 15, underscoring the importance of adhering to safety protocols in the operation and maintenance of high-pressure refrigeration systems.

The implementation of oxygen deprivation sensors in equipment rooms is part of a broader commitment to safety and environmental stewardship within the HVACR industry. These sensors are designed to detect the concentration of oxygen in the air, activating alarms when levels fall below a preset threshold, which is typically set at 19.5% oxygen by volume, as normal atmospheric air contains approximately 20.9% oxygen. This slight decrease can significantly impact human health, making the early detection of oxygen displacement critical. In addition to oxygen deprivation sensors, ASHRAE Standard 15 also outlines other safety measures, such as proper ventilation systems to dilute and remove refrigerants from the air, and the use of refrigerant detectors that can identify leaks of specific substances. These integrated safety systems work in tandem to provide a comprehensive safety net for technicians and others who work in or around equipment rooms, ensuring that the risks associated with refrigerant handling are minimized.

Chapter 3: Type 3 Low-Pressure Systems

Leak Detection

Leak Test Pressurization Methods

The hot water method or utilizing a built-in system heating/pressurization device such as Prevac stands as the most recommended approach for leak test pressurization in low-pressure systems. This method is preferred due to its efficiency in revealing leaks by creating a significant temperature difference across the system, which in turn, affects the pressure. The expansion and contraction of materials at different temperatures can help in identifying leaks more effectively. Moreover, the use of hot water or a heating device like Prevac ensures a uniform temperature distribution throughout the system, which is crucial for accurate leak detection. This method is particularly useful in environments where maintaining a controlled temperature is feasible and where the introduction of external gases like nitrogen might not be desirable due to contamination concerns or the potential for altering the chemical composition of the refrigerant or oil within the system.

Following the hot water method, the use of nitrogen as a pressurizing agent ranks second in the order of preference. Nitrogen is an inert gas, which makes it an excellent choice for pressurizing refrigeration systems without the risk of chemical reactions that could alter the properties of the refrigerant or the system itself. Its use is widespread in the industry due to its availability and the relative ease of handling. When introducing nitrogen into a low-pressure system, technicians can precisely control the pressure to simulate operational conditions or to stress test the system for leaks. This method is particularly advantageous when dealing with systems that cannot be easily or safely subjected to the hot water method, or in situations where the introduction of heat could compromise the integrity of the system components or the refrigerant.

Both methods have their specific applications and choosing between them depends on various factors including the system design, the refrigerant used, environmental conditions, and safety considerations. Technicians must be trained to understand the nuances of each method and to apply them appropriately based on the system they are working with. Proper application of these leak detection methods not only ensures compliance with environmental regulations but also contributes to the operational efficiency and longevity of the refrigeration systems.

Signs of Leakage in Low-Pressure Systems

Excessive purging in low-pressure systems often signals underlying issues, such as refrigerant leaks. This condition necessitates a thorough investigation to pinpoint the exact source of the leak. In low-pressure systems, leaks can lead to significant refrigerant loss, compromising system efficiency and environmental safety. Technicians should be vigilant for other signs that accompany excessive purging, including fluctuations in system pressure readings and unexplained loss of refrigerant charge. These symptoms may manifest subtly over time, requiring careful monitoring and diagnostic procedures to detect.

Identifying leaks in low-pressure systems involves a systematic approach, starting with visual inspections of all accessible components for signs of oil residue, which can indicate refrigerant leakage points. Since refrigerant and oil often escape together, oil traces can serve as a valuable clue. Additionally, employing electronic leak detectors around suspected areas can help in identifying the precise location of leaks. It's crucial for technicians to understand the behavior of low-pressure refrigerants and how leaks can vary in appearance and impact, depending on the system's specific configuration and the type of refrigerant used. Another critical aspect to consider is the condition of the system's seals and gaskets, as these components are common points of failure and potential leak sources. Over time, seals and gaskets may degrade, lose elasticity, or crack, allowing refrigerant to escape. Regular maintenance checks should include an assessment of these components' integrity to prevent leaks.

Technicians must also pay attention to the system's performance and operational data. An unexplained increase in energy consumption can indicate a system working harder to compensate for lost refrigerant, pointing to a potential leak. Similarly, inconsistent cooling performance or longer cycle times may suggest the system is not operating at optimal efficiency due to a refrigerant leak. Upon detecting a leak, immediate action is required to repair the leak point, followed by proper refrigerant recovery and system recharging according to EPA guidelines. This not only ensures the system returns to optimal operating conditions but also helps in minimizing environmental impact. Proper documentation of the leak detection process, repairs made, and refrigerant handling is essential for compliance with regulations and for future reference.

Technicians working with low-pressure systems must be equipped with the knowledge and tools necessary to effectively detect and address leaks. Continuous education on the latest refrigerant types, leak detection technologies, and repair techniques is vital for maintaining system integrity and environmental safety. By adopting a proactive approach to leak detection and repair, technicians can significantly reduce the incidence of excessive purging and its associated risks, ensuring the longevity and efficiency of low-pressure refrigeration systems.

Maximum Leak Test Pressure

When conducting leak tests on low-pressure centrifugal chillers, it's crucial to adhere to the maximum leak test pressure guidelines to prevent damage to the system. The maximum leak test pressure for these chillers is often set at a value that won't compromise the integrity of the chiller components, typically not exceeding 10 psig. This precaution is necessary because exceeding this pressure can lead to the deformation of seals, gaskets, and other critical components, which might not only cause immediate leaks but can also shorten the lifespan of the chiller.

It's important for technicians to use a calibrated pressure gauge to accurately measure the pressure during the test. The procedure should start with the system at its lowest possible pressure point, gradually increasing the pressure until it reaches the test limit. This methodical approach allows for the detection of leaks without stressing the system unnecessarily.

Technicians must also ensure that the pressure is applied uniformly across the system to avoid localized stress points that could lead to false readings or damage. The use of nitrogen, due to its inert properties, is recommended for this process. Nitrogen can safely pressurize the system without reacting with the refrigerant or the oil within the chiller. Furthermore, understanding the specific design and operational parameters of the low-pressure centrifugal chiller in question is essential. Each chiller model may have its own manufacturer-recommended maximum leak test pressure, which could differ from the general guideline. Therefore, consulting the manufacturer's documentation or technical support team before performing a leak test is advisable.

Leak Inspection for High Leak Rate

For appliances that exceed the leak rate, stringent leak inspection requirements come into play to ensure environmental safety and system efficiency. The Environmental Protection Agency (EPA) mandates that any appliance exceeding the prescribed leak rate must undergo a thorough inspection to identify and rectify the source of the leaks. This process is critical, not only for compliance with regulations but also for the preservation of the ozone layer and the prevention of global warming. The first step in this process involves a detailed assessment of the appliance to pinpoint the exact locations of leaks. Technicians must employ a variety of methods, including **electronic leak detection**, **ultrasonic leak detection**, and **fluorescent dye injection**, to ensure that no leak is overlooked. Each of these methods has its own set of advantages and is selected based on the appliance's specific characteristics and the nature of the refrigerant used.

Electronic leak detectors are highly sensitive and can detect minute leaks that might not be visible to the naked eye. They are particularly useful for initial screenings and for checking areas that are known to be prone to leaks, such as joints and connections. **Ultrasonic leak detectors**, on the other hand, identify leaks by detecting the sound of the refrigerant escaping from the system. This method is beneficial for locating leaks in noisy environments where other detectors might not be as effective. **Fluorescent dye injection** involves adding a special dye to the refrigerant, which circulates through the system. The dye escapes with the refrigerant at leak points, and under a UV light, these leaks become visible. This method is especially useful for complex systems where leaks are difficult to locate. Once leaks are identified, it is imperative to repair them promptly to prevent further refrigerant loss. The EPA requires that repairs be completed within a specific timeframe, depending on the type of appliance and the amount of refrigerant it contains. After repairs are made, the appliance must be retested to ensure that it no longer exceeds the leak rate. This retesting is crucial for verifying the effectiveness of the repairs and for documenting compliance with EPA regulations.

Documentation plays a significant role in the leak inspection process. Technicians must maintain detailed records of the inspection, including the methods used to detect leaks, the locations of the leaks, the repairs performed, and the results of the retesting. These records are essential for demonstrating compliance with EPA regulations and for tracking the appliance's leak history over time. In addition to repairing leaks, technicians must also consider the overall condition of the appliance and recommend any necessary upgrades or replacements that could prevent future leaks. This might include replacing outdated components with more modern, leak-resistant versions or retrofitting the appliance to use a refrigerant with a lower global warming potential (GWP). For appliances that repeatedly exceed the leak rate despite repairs, more drastic measures may be required. The EPA mandates that appliances that cannot be repaired to comply with the leak rate must be retired and properly disposed of to prevent further environmental damage. This decision is not taken lightly and is considered a last resort after all other options have been exhausted. Technicians working with appliances that exceed the leak rate must be thoroughly trained in leak detection and repair techniques. They must also be familiar with the EPA regulations governing leak inspection and repair to ensure that their work complies with federal requirements. Continuous education and training are essential for staying up-to-date with the latest technologies and regulations in the field.

Leak Repair Requirements

Annual Leak Rate for Refrigeration

The Environmental Protection Agency (EPA) has set forth specific regulations concerning the allowable annual leak rate for commercial and industrial process refrigeration systems. These guidelines are critical for technicians and facility managers to understand and adhere to, ensuring both compliance with legal standards and the protection of the environment from the harmful effects of refrigerant leaks. The allowable annual leak rate for commercial and industrial process refrigeration systems is pegged at 35 percent. This threshold is designed to prompt immediate action in the event of a leak, necessitating repairs to bring the system back into compliance and reduce the potential for ozone depletion and global warming.

For systems containing more than 50 pounds of refrigerant, the detection and repair of leaks become even more critical. When a system is found to exceed this 35 percent leak rate, operators are required to conduct repairs within 30 days of detection, unless an extension is granted under specific circumstances. Following the repair, it is mandatory to conduct a verification test to ensure the effectiveness of the repair within another 30 days. This rigorous approach underscores the EPA's commitment to minimizing the environmental impact of refrigerant emissions.

Technicians play a pivotal role in this process, requiring a deep understanding of leak detection methods, repair techniques, and the proper documentation of all actions taken. The use of advanced leak detection technologies, such as infrared imaging and ultrasonic detectors, enhances the ability to identify leaks with greater accuracy and speed, thereby facilitating timely repairs. Moreover, the selection of appropriate repair methods, whether it involves replacing faulty components or sealing leaks, is crucial for restoring system integrity and compliance. Documentation is another critical aspect of managing the allowable annual leak rate. Detailed records must be maintained, including the dates of leak detection, the methods used for detection, the specific repairs carried out, and the results of the verification test. This documentation not only serves as evidence of compliance with EPA regulations but also provides valuable data for analyzing the performance and reliability of refrigeration systems over time. Training and certification in accordance with EPA guidelines are essential for technicians working with commercial and industrial process refrigeration systems. This ensures that they are equipped with the latest knowledge and skills to effectively manage refrigerant leaks and adhere to environmental regulations. Continuous education on evolving refrigerant technologies and regulations is also vital, as it enables technicians to stay abreast of best practices and emerging trends in refrigerant management.

The management of allowable annual leak rates is a shared responsibility, involving technicians, facility managers, and regulatory bodies. By working collaboratively, these stakeholders can significantly reduce the environmental impact of refrigerant leaks, ensuring the sustainability of commercial and industrial refrigeration systems. This collective effort not only aids in compliance with legal standards but also contributes to the broader goal of protecting the environment for future generations.

Annual Leak Rate for Large Appliances

For appliances containing more than 50 pounds of refrigerant, the Environmental Protection Agency (EPA) has set forth specific regulations to manage and mitigate the environmental impact of refrigerant leaks. These regulations are part of a broader effort to preserve the ozone layer and reduce global warming potential by minimizing the release of ozone-depleting substances and high global warming potential refrigerants into the atmosphere. The allowable annual leak rate for these larger systems is a critical component of these regulations, designed to prompt timely repairs and ensure system integrity.

The EPA mandates that owners or operators of commercial refrigeration and air conditioning equipment containing more than 50 pounds of refrigerant must conduct regular leak inspections and repair any leaks within a specified timeframe. The allowable annual leak rate for these appliances is set at 30% for industrial process refrigeration (IPR) and commercial refrigeration equipment, and 10% for comfort cooling equipment. This distinction underscores the varying impact and usage patterns of refrigeration equipment across different sectors. To comply with these regulations, operators must calculate the leak rate annually by comparing the quantity of refrigerant added to the appliance to the appliance's full charge. If the leak rate exceeds the allowable threshold, the operator is required to take corrective action to repair the leaks. This process not only involves identifying and fixing the leaks but also verifying that the repairs have effectively reduced the leak rate below the allowable limit. Following the repair, a follow-up verification test is required within 30 days to ensure the leak has been adequately addressed.

Documentation plays a crucial role in compliance with EPA regulations. Operators must maintain detailed records of all leak inspections, repairs, and verifications for at least three years. These records must include the dates of discovery and repair of leaks, the location of leaks within the system, the type and quantity of refrigerant added, and the methods used to verify repairs. In addition to regular leak inspections, the EPA's regulations encourage the adoption of best practices in system management and maintenance. This includes the implementation of leak detection technologies, regular maintenance schedules, and technician training programs. By proactively managing refrigeration systems and promptly addressing leaks, operators can not only comply with regulatory requirements but also improve system efficiency, reduce operating costs, and minimize environmental impact.

The focus on reducing the allowable annual leak rate for appliances with more than 50 pounds of refrigerant reflects the EPA's commitment to environmental protection. It aligns with global efforts under the Montreal Protocol to phase down the use and production of ozone-depleting substances and transition to more sustainable refrigeration technologies.

Recovery Techniques

Speeding Up Liquid Recovery Process

Recovering liquid refrigerant at the beginning of the recovery process is a critical technique for technicians working with Type 3 Low-Pressure Systems. This method significantly accelerates the recovery process by taking advantage of the physical properties of refrigerants. Liquid refrigerant has a much higher density than its vapor form, allowing for a more efficient transfer out of the system. By focusing on liquid recovery first, technicians can remove a substantial portion of the refrigerant quickly, reducing the overall time required for the process.

To effectively implement this technique, it is essential to understand the configuration of the refrigeration system and identify the points where liquid refrigerant is likely to accumulate. Typically, this includes the receiver and the lowest points of the system where refrigerant settles due to gravity. The use of specialized recovery equipment designed for low-pressure systems is also crucial. This equipment must be capable of handling the system's pressures and temperatures without compromising safety or efficiency.

Once the liquid refrigerant has been successfully recovered, the focus shifts to the vapor phase. The remaining vapor is removed using a vacuum pump, which lowers the pressure within the system, causing the refrigerant to evaporate more rapidly. This step is vital for ensuring that the system is completely free of refrigerant, allowing for safe repairs, maintenance, or disposal of the equipment. Technicians must also be mindful of environmental regulations and safety protocols throughout the recovery process. The Clean Air Act and EPA regulations mandate specific procedures for the recovery and disposal of refrigerants to prevent their release into the atmosphere. Proper training and certification in these procedures are mandatory for all technicians to ensure compliance and protect the environment. Furthermore, understanding the characteristics of the refrigerant being recovered, such as its boiling point and pressure-temperature relationship, is essential for optimizing the recovery process. This knowledge allows technicians to adjust their equipment settings and procedures to match the specific requirements of each refrigerant type, enhancing efficiency and safety. In addition to environmental and regulatory considerations, the economic aspects of refrigerant recovery cannot be overlooked. Recovering refrigerant as a liquid not only speeds up the process but also minimizes the loss of refrigerant. This efficiency can lead to cost savings for HVACR service companies and their clients, as less refrigerant needs to be replaced. Moreover, recovered refrigerant that meets purity standards can be reclaimed and reused, further reducing costs and environmental impact.

Recovering Vapor and Liquid

After the liquid refrigerant has been successfully removed from the system, the recovery process must then focus on the vapor phase to ensure complete evacuation of the refrigerant. This step is crucial for several reasons, primarily to prevent any residual refrigerant from escaping into the atmosphere, which could contribute to ozone depletion or global warming. The process of vapor recovery involves creating a vacuum within the system that lowers the pressure, encouraging the remaining refrigerant to evaporate more quickly. This method is effective in removing the last traces of refrigerant, which are often the most challenging to capture due to their gaseous state.

To optimize the vapor recovery process, technicians must employ a vacuum pump capable of achieving a deep vacuum, typically in the range of 500 microns or lower. This level of vacuum ensures that even the most stubborn refrigerant vapors are extracted from the system. It's important for technicians to monitor the vacuum level closely, using a reliable vacuum gauge to detect any potential leaks within the system that could hinder the recovery process. Identifying and addressing these leaks is essential for maintaining the integrity of the system and ensuring that it is properly prepared for subsequent repairs or refrigerant recharge.

The duration of the vacuum process can vary depending on the size and complexity of the system, as well as the type of refrigerant being recovered. Technicians should refer to the manufacturer's specifications and EPA guidelines to determine the appropriate vacuum level and recovery time for each specific scenario. Additionally, ambient temperature can affect the vapor recovery process, with warmer conditions potentially speeding up the evaporation of the refrigerant. Technicians may need to adjust their approach based on environmental factors to achieve the most efficient recovery. Safety precautions are paramount during the vapor recovery phase, as exposure to refrigerant vapors can pose health risks to technicians. Proper personal protective equipment, including gloves and goggles, should be worn at all times, and adequate ventilation should be ensured to minimize the inhalation of fumes. Furthermore, technicians must be trained in the proper handling and disposal of refrigerants to comply with environmental regulations and prevent any adverse impact on the environment.

The final step in the vapor recovery process involves verifying that the system has been completely evacuated of refrigerant. This can be achieved through the use of a refrigerant identifier, which analyzes the composition of the gases within the system to ensure that no refrigerant remains. This verification step is critical for ensuring compliance with EPA regulations, which mandate the complete recovery of refrigerants to prevent their release into the atmosphere. By meticulously following the vapor recovery process, technicians can ensure that Type 3 Low-Pressure Systems are properly serviced and maintained, contributing to the overall efficiency and longevity of the equipment. This attention to detail not only helps protect the environment by preventing the release of harmful refrigerants but also ensures that systems are prepared for safe and effective operation. The skills and knowledge required for effective vapor recovery are essential components of a technician's expertise, underscoring the importance of comprehensive training and certification in the field of HVACR.

Heating Oil to 130°F for Safety

Heating oil to 130°F before its removal is a critical step in the refrigerant recovery process for Type 3 Low-Pressure Systems, primarily aimed at minimizing refrigerant release. This procedure ensures that the oil, which can absorb and retain refrigerant, is purged of as much refrigerant as possible by utilizing heat to lower the refrigerant's solubility in the oil. The significance of this step cannot be overstated, as it directly impacts the efficiency of the recovery process and the environmental footprint of the operation. The heating of oil to this specific temperature leverages the physical properties of the refrigerant, promoting its transition from a dissolved state within the oil to a gaseous state that can be more easily extracted through the recovery system.

The methodology for heating oil to the optimal temperature of 130°F involves careful monitoring to avoid overheating, which could degrade the oil or release harmful compounds. Technicians must employ precise temperature control mechanisms and continuously monitor the oil's temperature throughout the process. This may involve the use of specialized equipment designed to evenly distribute heat and prevent hot spots that could damage the oil or the system components. In addition to the technical aspects of heating oil, safety considerations must also be paramount. Technicians should wear appropriate personal protective equipment to guard against burns from hot oil or any accidental release of refrigerant that may occur during the heating process. Ventilation is another critical factor, as the heating process can potentially release volatile compounds into the air. Ensuring a well-ventilated workspace is essential to maintain a safe environment for the technician and prevent the accumulation of any potentially harmful gases.

The rationale behind heating oil to 130°F ties back to the overarching goal of maximizing the recovery of refrigerant and minimizing its release into the atmosphere. By reducing the refrigerant content in the oil, technicians can ensure that the system is thoroughly evacuated of refrigerant, aligning with environmental regulations and best practices. This step is particularly crucial for systems that have been in service for extended periods, as the accumulation of refrigerant in the oil can be significant. Furthermore, the process of heating the oil and removing the refrigerant is not only a regulatory requirement but also a measure that enhances the overall performance and longevity of the refrigeration system. Clean oil, free of refrigerant, ensures better lubrication and reduces the wear and tear on system components, leading to more efficient operation and reduced maintenance costs over time.

Technicians undertaking this procedure must be well-versed in the specific requirements of the refrigerants and oils they are working with, as different types may have varying solubility characteristics and temperature sensitivities. Knowledge of the refrigerant's pressure-temperature relationship is also essential, as it informs the technician of the conditions under which the refrigerant will be released from the oil.

In practice, the heating of oil to 130°F before removal is a testament to the meticulous and environmentally responsible approach required in the field of HVACR. It exemplifies the technical proficiency and environmental stewardship that technicians must embody, ensuring that every step of the refrigerant recovery process is conducted with precision and care for the environment. This procedure, while seemingly straightforward, encapsulates the complex interplay between thermodynamics, environmental science, and practical HVACR expertise, underscoring the importance of comprehensive training and certification in the field.

Prevent Freezing During Refrigerant Evacuation

The necessity to circulate or remove water from the chiller during refrigerant evacuation is a critical step to prevent the freezing of water within the system. This process is particularly important in Type 3 Low-Pressure Systems, where the refrigerant operates at temperatures that can easily freeze water, potentially causing significant damage to the chiller's components. The presence of water in the system during evacuation can lead to ice formation, which may block the flow of refrigerant and impede the efficiency of the recovery process. Moreover, ice can exert pressure on the pipes and components of the chiller, leading to cracks or breaks that could compromise the integrity of the system. To mitigate these risks, technicians must employ strategies to either circulate the water to maintain it above freezing temperatures or completely remove it from the system prior to the start of the refrigerant evacuation process. Circulating the water can be achieved by using the chiller's built-in pumps or by temporarily installing external pumps to keep the water moving. This movement of water helps to prevent the formation of ice by continuously transferring heat within the system and maintaining the water at a temperature above its freezing point.

In scenarios where circulating the water is not feasible or practical, the complete removal of water from the system is the preferred approach. This can be accomplished by draining the water from the chiller and all associated components before beginning the refrigerant evacuation. It is crucial that technicians ensure all water is thoroughly removed to avoid any residual moisture that could freeze during the evacuation process. Technicians must also consider the ambient temperature conditions when performing these procedures, as colder environmental temperatures can accelerate the freezing process, necessitating more rigorous measures to prevent ice formation. Additionally, the specific design and configuration of the chiller system may influence the choice of method for managing water during refrigerant evacuation. It is essential for technicians to consult the manufacturer's guidelines and specifications to determine the most effective and safe approach for each particular system.

The importance of preventing water freezing during refrigerant evacuation extends beyond the immediate risk of physical damage to the chiller. Ice formation can also lead to incomplete recovery of refrigerant, as blockages can prevent the full evacuation of the system. This not only poses environmental risks due to potential refrigerant leakage but also violates EPA regulations that mandate complete recovery of refrigerants to minimize their release into the atmosphere. Therefore, the proper management of water in the chiller during refrigerant evacuation is not only a matter of mechanical integrity but also of regulatory compliance and environmental responsibility. In practice, the steps taken to circulate or remove water from the chiller must be carefully planned and executed as part of the overall refrigerant recovery strategy. This requires a comprehensive understanding of the system's design, the physical properties of the refrigerant and water, and the environmental conditions at the time of recovery. Technicians must be adept at adapting their approach to suit the specific circumstances of each chiller system, ensuring that the refrigerant evacuation process is conducted efficiently, safely, and in accordance with all applicable standards and regulations. This level of expertise underscores the importance of thorough training and certification for technicians working with Type 3 Low-Pressure Systems, equipping them with the knowledge and skills necessary to navigate the complexities of refrigerant recovery and system maintenance.

High-Pressure Cut-Out in Recovery Devices

The high-pressure cut-out level of recovery devices used with low-pressure appliances is a critical safety feature designed to prevent the over-pressurization of the recovery tank and the potential for the refrigerant recovery machine to operate beyond its safe operating limits. This feature is particularly important in the context of Type 3 Low-Pressure Systems, where the refrigerants used have a lower pressure at room temperature compared to high-pressure systems. The high-pressure cut-out setting must be carefully selected based on the specifications of the recovery machine and the characteristics of the refrigerant being recovered. It acts as a safeguard, automatically shutting off the recovery machine if the pressure in the recovery tank reaches a level that could pose a risk of tank rupture or damage to the recovery machine.

For technicians working with Type 3 Low-Pressure Systems, understanding the correct high-pressure cut-out setting is essential. This setting varies depending on the type of refrigerant and the design of the recovery equipment. Manufacturers of recovery machines typically provide guidelines on the appropriate settings for different refrigerants. It is imperative that technicians refer to these guidelines and adjust the high-pressure cut-out setting accordingly before beginning the recovery process. Failure to do so can result in equipment damage, safety hazards, and non-compliance with environmental regulations. The selection of the high-pressure cut-out level is also influenced by ambient temperature conditions, as the pressure of the refrigerant within the recovery tank will increase with temperature. Technicians must account for the potential for ambient temperature fluctuations, especially when recovering refrigerant in outdoor environments or in spaces where temperature control is not stable. In some cases, it may be necessary to adjust the high-pressure cut-out setting mid-operation if there is a significant change in ambient temperature.

Moreover, the high-pressure cut-out feature plays a crucial role in ensuring the integrity of the recovery process. By preventing over-pressurization, it helps to minimize the risk of refrigerant leaks during recovery, thereby supporting the goals of environmental protection and regulatory compliance. Leaks not only result in the loss of refrigerant but also contribute to the emission of greenhouse gases and substances that can deplete the ozone layer. Therefore, the proper setting of the high-pressure cut-out level is not just a matter of operational safety but also an environmental imperative. In addition to setting the high-pressure cut-out level, technicians must regularly inspect and maintain recovery equipment to ensure that all safety features, including the high-pressure cut-out mechanism, are functioning correctly. Regular maintenance checks should include verifying the accuracy of pressure gauges, inspecting hoses and connections for signs of wear or damage, and testing the high-pressure cut-out feature to confirm that it activates at the set point. These preventive measures are essential for maintaining the safety and efficiency of the refrigerant recovery process.

The high-pressure cut-out level is a key component of the recovery equipment's safety system, designed to protect both the technician and the environment. By adhering to manufacturer guidelines and best practices for setting and maintaining this feature, technicians can ensure that refrigerant recovery operations are conducted safely, efficiently, and in compliance with environmental regulations. This attention to detail reflects the professional standards expected of HVACR technicians and underscores the importance of comprehensive training and certification in the field.

Recharging Techniques

Prevent Freezing: Vapor Before Liquid

Introducing vapor before liquid into the system is a critical step in the recharging process for Type 3 Low-Pressure Systems, primarily to prevent the freezing of water in the tubes, which can cause significant damage and inefficiency in the system. This technique is essential for maintaining the integrity of the refrigeration cycle and ensuring that the system operates at optimal levels without causing undue stress on the components. The process begins with the careful introduction of vapor refrigerant into the system, which allows for a gradual increase in pressure and temperature. This step is crucial for pre-warming the tubes and components, thereby mitigating the risk of thermal shock and freezing that can occur if liquid refrigerant were introduced too rapidly.

The vapor introduction phase should be monitored closely, with technicians paying attention to the system's pressure and temperature readings. It is imperative to achieve a balance that warms up the system sufficiently without causing excessive pressure build-up, which could lead to other complications. Once the system has been adequately preconditioned with vapor, the technician can then proceed to introduce the liquid refrigerant. This methodical approach ensures that the refrigerant absorbs heat from the surrounding components and the water in the tubes, thus preventing any freezing from occurring. Furthermore, this technique underscores the importance of understanding the physical properties of refrigerants and their behavior under different pressures and temperatures. Technicians must be well-versed in the phase change characteristics of the refrigerant being used, as well as the specific requirements of the system they are working on. This knowledge is critical in determining the appropriate amounts of vapor and liquid refrigerant to introduce, as well as the timing of each phase of the recharging process.

In addition to preventing freezing, the careful management of vapor and liquid phases during recharging plays a vital role in achieving efficient heat exchange within the system. It ensures that the refrigerant is evenly distributed throughout the system, maximizing contact with the heat exchange surfaces and facilitating optimal thermal transfer. This efficiency not only enhances the performance of the system but also contributes to energy conservation and the overall sustainability of the operation.

Technicians must also be aware of the environmental implications of their work, especially in the context of Type 3 Low-Pressure Systems, which often use refrigerants with significant global warming potential. The meticulous approach to recharging, focusing on the prevention of freezing and the efficient use of refrigerant, aligns with broader environmental goals by minimizing leaks and reducing the system's carbon footprint. In practice, the recharging process requires a combination of technical skill, theoretical knowledge, and practical experience. Technicians should employ the use of specialized tools and equipment, such as refrigerant recovery units and charging scales, to accurately measure and control the flow of refrigerant into the system. Additionally, adherence to safety protocols cannot be overstated, as the handling of refrigerants poses potential risks to both the technician and the environment. Proper personal protective equipment, such as gloves and goggles, should be worn at all times, and technicians should be trained in the safe handling and disposal of refrigerants.

Overall, the introduction of vapor before liquid is a nuanced procedure that exemplifies the technical complexity of servicing Type 3 Low-Pressure Systems. It highlights the need for a thorough understanding of refrigeration principles, meticulous attention to detail, and a commitment to environmental stewardship. By mastering this technique, technicians can ensure the longevity and efficiency of the systems they service, while also contributing to the broader goals of energy conservation and environmental protection.

Charging Centrifugals via Evaporator Valve

Charging centrifugal chillers through the evaporator charging valve is a critical procedure that demands precision and adherence to specific guidelines to ensure the system's efficiency and longevity. This method involves introducing the refrigerant into the chiller's evaporator section, where it is crucial for the refrigerant to be in the correct state to facilitate optimal heat exchange and prevent any potential damage to the system. The evaporator charging valve is designed to control the flow of refrigerant, allowing for a more accurate and controlled charge, which is essential for maintaining the balance within the system.

When charging through the evaporator charging valve, technicians must monitor the system's pressure and temperature closely. The goal is to achieve a precise balance that ensures the refrigerant is introduced at a rate that the system can effectively manage, avoiding any sudden changes that could disrupt the operation or cause damage. This process requires a deep understanding of the system's design and the characteristics of the refrigerant being used. Knowledge of the specific pressure-temperature relationship of the refrigerant is crucial, as this will guide the technician in determining the correct amount of refrigerant to introduce and the rate at which to do so. Furthermore, the technique of charging through the evaporator charging valve underscores the importance of precision in the refrigeration field. It highlights the need for technicians to be meticulous in their approach, using accurate instruments to measure the refrigerant quantity and closely observing the system's response throughout the process. This method not only ensures the system's efficiency but also emphasizes the technician's role in safeguarding the environment by preventing the unnecessary release of refrigerants.

Technicians must also be aware of the safety protocols associated with handling refrigerants, including the use of appropriate personal protective equipment and the proper disposal of any refrigerant waste. The procedure of charging through the evaporator charging valve is a testament to the intricate balance required in refrigeration systems, where every step taken affects the system's performance and environmental impact.

Recovery Requirements

Evacuation for Low-Pressure Disposal

The evacuation requirements for low-pressure appliances during disposal are critical to ensuring environmental safety and compliance with federal regulations. The Environmental Protection Agency (EPA) mandates specific procedures to minimize the release of refrigerants into the atmosphere, which can contribute to ozone depletion and global warming. For low-pressure systems, particularly those being prepared for disposal, technicians must adhere to stringent evacuation standards to remove refrigerants effectively.

Before disposal, all refrigerants must be evacuated from the appliance to levels that meet or exceed EPA-established thresholds. For low-pressure systems, this means achieving a vacuum of 25 microns (0.033 mbar) to ensure that virtually all the refrigerant has been removed. Achieving such a low level of vacuum requires the use of high-quality vacuum pumps and accurate micron gauges to monitor the evacuation process. It is imperative that technicians verify the vacuum level has been maintained for a minimum period, as specified by the EPA, to confirm that the refrigerant has been adequately removed. The process of evacuating refrigerant from low-pressure systems involves several steps, beginning with the proper identification and recovery of the refrigerant. Technicians must use recovery machines designed for low-pressure refrigerants, which are capable of handling the appliance's specific refrigerant type without causing cross-contamination. Following the recovery phase, the system must be evacuated using a vacuum pump rated for deep vacuum operation. During this phase, it's crucial to monitor the system for any signs of leaks, as any breach could allow air and moisture to enter, compromising the evacuation process and potentially damaging the system. Technicians must also be mindful of the oil in the system, which can retain significant amounts of refrigerant. Heating the oil to at least 130°F (54°C) can help release trapped refrigerant, facilitating its removal during the evacuation process. This step is particularly important in low-pressure systems, where refrigerant solubility in oil is high. The careful management of oil temperatures and the use of appropriate heating methods are essential to ensure complete refrigerant removal.

Furthermore, the evacuation of refrigerant from low-pressure appliances requires a thorough understanding of the system's design and the behavior of low-pressure refrigerants under various conditions. Technicians must be equipped with knowledge and tools to adapt the evacuation process to the specific requirements of each appliance, taking into account factors such as the refrigerant type, the quantity of refrigerant and oil in the system, and the ambient temperature conditions.

In addition to technical proficiency, adherence to safety protocols is paramount during the evacuation process. Technicians must wear appropriate personal protective equipment (PPE) and follow best practices for handling refrigerants and operating recovery and evacuation equipment. The safe and effective evacuation of refrigerants from low-pressure systems is not only a matter of regulatory compliance but also a reflection of the technician's commitment to environmental stewardship and professional responsibility. As the final step before disposal, the evacuation of refrigerants from low-pressure appliances underscores the importance of meticulous attention to detail, advanced technical skills, and a deep understanding of environmental regulations. By following the EPA's stringent evacuation requirements, technicians play a crucial role in protecting the environment and ensuring the safe disposal of low-pressure appliances.

Evacuation for Low-Pressure Repairs

The distinction between major and non-major repairs in the context of low-pressure appliances significantly influences the evacuation requirements set forth by the Environmental Protection Agency (EPA). For major repairs, which typically involve the disassembly of an appliance or the disturbance of its refrigerant circuit, the EPA mandates a thorough evacuation to ensure that no refrigerant escapes into the atmosphere. This process is critical, as it directly impacts the environmental footprint of HVACR service practices. The evacuation must reach a vacuum level sufficient to remove virtually all the refrigerant from the system. Technicians are required to achieve a vacuum of 25 microns (0.033 mbar), a standard that underscores the importance of using high-quality vacuum pumps and accurate micron gauges to monitor the evacuation process meticulously.

In contrast, the evacuation requirements for non-major repairs, which might include tasks that do not involve opening the refrigerant circuit, such as external electrical repairs or mechanical maintenance, are less stringent. For these types of repairs, the primary goal is to ensure that the system is free of non-condensables and that any potential for refrigerant leakage is minimized. However, the full evacuation to the 25-micron level is not always necessary, provided that the integrity of the refrigerant circuit remains uncompromised. The focus for non-major repairs is on maintaining system efficiency and preventing any indirect environmental harm that could arise from decreased performance or potential leaks. The procedural differences in evacuation for major versus non-major repairs highlight the nuanced understanding required by technicians to navigate EPA regulations effectively. For major repairs, the evacuation process often involves several stages, including the initial recovery of refrigerant into a recovery cylinder, followed by the use of a vacuum pump to achieve the required vacuum level. This process may be time-consuming but is essential for ensuring compliance with environmental regulations and for safeguarding the integrity of the refrigerant system. Technicians must be vigilant in monitoring the system for leaks during and after the evacuation process, as any breach could compromise the repair and lead to environmental harm.

For non-major repairs, while the full evacuation process may not be necessary, technicians must still exercise caution to avoid releasing refrigerants into the atmosphere. This includes conducting a thorough leak check before and after the repair process and ensuring that any connections to the refrigerant circuit are properly sealed. The approach to non-major repairs emphasizes the importance of preventive maintenance and the role of technicians in identifying potential issues before they necessitate major repairs. Both major and non-major repairs require a deep understanding of the refrigeration system being serviced, including knowledge of the specific type of low-pressure refrigerant used, the system's design, and the potential environmental impacts of the refrigerant. Technicians must also be proficient in the use of recovery and evacuation equipment, ensuring that they can effectively remove refrigerant from the system without causing cross-contamination or harm to the environment.

The EPA's stringent requirements for the evacuation of refrigerants from low-pressure appliances during both major and non-major repairs reflect the agency's commitment to environmental protection. By adhering to these requirements, technicians play a vital role in minimizing the release of ozone-depleting substances and greenhouse gases, contributing to the global effort to combat climate change and protect the ozone layer. The distinction between major and non-major repairs underscores the need for technicians to be adaptable, knowledgeable, and conscientious in their work, balancing the technical demands of their profession with the broader environmental responsibilities that come with handling refrigerants.

Evacuation for Leaky vs. Non-Leaky Appliances

The evacuation requirements for low-pressure appliances, when considering leaky versus non-leaky systems, necessitate a detailed understanding of the procedures that ensure the safe and effective removal of refrigerants. For appliances identified as leaky, the urgency and methodology of the evacuation process are significantly heightened compared to their non-leaky counterparts. This distinction is crucial for technicians aiming to adhere to both environmental regulations and best practices in HVACR system maintenance.

Leaky low-pressure appliances present a unique challenge due to the potential for refrigerant loss to the atmosphere, which can contribute to ozone depletion and global warming. The Environmental Protection Agency (EPA) mandates that technicians must perform a thorough evacuation to a vacuum level of 25 microns (0.033 mbar) to ensure the removal of as much refrigerant as possible before any repair or disposal actions. This standard is critical in preventing the escape of harmful substances and underscores the need for precise and reliable vacuum equipment. Technicians must also be vigilant in detecting and repairing leaks before proceeding with the evacuation, as unresolved leaks can compromise the effectiveness of the process and lead to further environmental harm. In contrast, non-leaky low-pressure appliances do not pose the same immediate risk of refrigerant release. However, the evacuation process remains a critical step in maintaining system integrity and performance. For these systems, the evacuation requirements focus on ensuring that no non-condensables or moisture remain within the system, which can affect efficiency and lead to potential damage. While the vacuum level required may be the same, the approach to achieving it can be adjusted based on the condition of the appliance and the absence of leaks. This adjustment is a testament to the technician's ability to apply their knowledge and skills flexibly, based on the specific circumstances of each appliance.

The distinction between leaky and non-leaky low-pressure appliances also highlights the importance of accurate and sensitive leak detection methods. Technicians must employ a range of techniques, from electronic detectors to soap bubble tests, to identify leaks with precision. The identification process is not only a prerequisite for effective evacuation but also a critical component of environmental stewardship, ensuring that repairs are carried out in a manner that minimizes the potential for refrigerant release. Moreover, the evacuation process, whether for leaky or non-leaky appliances, must be documented meticulously. This documentation serves as a record of compliance with EPA regulations and as a valuable resource for future maintenance and service interventions. It includes details of the evacuation procedure, vacuum levels achieved, leak detection and repair activities, and any refrigerant recovery or recycling actions taken. This comprehensive approach to documentation reinforces the accountability of technicians and their role in promoting sustainable practices within the HVACR industry.

Technicians working on low-pressure systems must also consider the specific characteristics of the refrigerants involved, as these can influence the evacuation process. Low-pressure refrigerants, such as R-123 or R-11, have distinct properties that require specialized handling and recovery techniques. Understanding these properties is essential for technicians to perform evacuations effectively, ensuring that all refrigerant is removed from the system without causing damage or environmental harm.

The need for specialized training and continuous education is evident in the context of evacuating leaky versus non-leaky low-pressure appliances. Technicians must stay informed about the latest tools, techniques, and regulations to navigate the complexities of the evacuation process successfully. This ongoing learning process is not only a professional requirement but also a reflection of the technician's commitment to excellence and environmental responsibility. In handling low-pressure appliances, whether leaky or non-leaky, technicians are tasked with a significant responsibility. The evacuation process is a critical step in ensuring the safe, efficient, and environmentally friendly operation of HVACR systems. By adhering to stringent evacuation requirements and employing best practices in leak detection and repair, technicians uphold the highest standards of professional conduct and contribute to the broader goals of environmental protection and sustainability.

Evacuation for Low-Pressure Appliances

The evacuation requirements for low-pressure appliances, particularly when considering the appliance or component containing less versus more than 200 pounds of refrigerant, necessitate a nuanced approach to ensure both environmental safety and regulatory compliance. The Environmental Protection Agency (EPA) has established specific protocols to guide technicians through the correct evacuation process, tailored to the quantity of refrigerant within the system. For appliances containing less than 200 pounds of refrigerant, the focus is on achieving a thorough evacuation to a vacuum level that ensures the removal of the majority of the refrigerant, thereby minimizing the potential for ozone depletion and global warming contributions. This typically involves reaching a vacuum of 25 microns (0.033 mbar), which effectively removes the refrigerant to levels that significantly reduce environmental risk. Conversely, for appliances or components containing more than 200 pounds of refrigerant, the evacuation requirements become more stringent. The rationale behind this is the greater environmental impact associated with the release of larger quantities of refrigerant. In these cases, technicians are required to employ more sophisticated recovery and evacuation equipment capable of achieving deeper vacuum levels. This ensures that a higher percentage of the refrigerant is recovered, thereby further mitigating the potential for environmental harm. The process for these larger systems often involves a series of steps that include the initial recovery of refrigerant into a recovery cylinder, followed by the use of a vacuum pump to achieve the required deep vacuum level. Throughout this process, it is crucial for technicians to monitor the system meticulously for any signs of leaks or system breaches that could compromise the evacuation process. The differentiation in evacuation requirements based on the amount of refrigerant present underscores the importance of accurate refrigerant management practices. Technicians must be adept at identifying the type and quantity of refrigerant in the system before beginning the evacuation process. This not only ensures compliance with EPA regulations but also promotes the efficient use of resources and time during the recovery and evacuation phases. The use of precise measuring tools and scales is essential in this regard, allowing technicians to accurately gauge the amount of refrigerant to be recovered and to adjust their evacuation strategies accordingly.

Moreover, the emphasis on deeper vacuum levels for systems with more than 200 pounds of refrigerant highlights the critical role of high-quality vacuum pumps and micron gauges in the HVACR industry. These tools enable technicians to achieve and verify the vacuum levels required by the EPA, ensuring that the evacuation process is both effective and compliant with environmental regulations. The selection of appropriate recovery and evacuation equipment is thus a key factor in the successful management of low-pressure systems, particularly those containing significant amounts of refrigerant.

In addition to the technical aspects of the evacuation process, technicians must also prioritize safety and environmental protection throughout. This includes the proper handling and disposal of recovered refrigerants, adherence to safety protocols to protect both the technician and the environment, and the meticulous documentation of the evacuation process. Documentation plays a pivotal role in demonstrating compliance with EPA regulations and in maintaining accurate records for future reference and regulatory audits. The detailed approach to evacuation requirements for low-pressure appliances, based on the quantity of refrigerant, reflects the EPA's commitment to minimizing the environmental impact of refrigerant emissions. It also underscores the need for technicians to possess a comprehensive understanding of refrigerant management practices, the technical skills to implement them effectively, and a strong commitment to environmental stewardship.

Evacuation for Pre/Post-1993 Equipment

For low-pressure appliances, the evacuation requirements significantly differ based on whether the recovery/recycling equipment was manufactured before or after November 15, 1993. This distinction is crucial due to the advancements in technology and regulatory standards that have occurred over time, impacting the efficiency and environmental safety of the recovery process.

Recovery and recycling equipment built before November 15, 1993, often lacks the precision and efficiency found in newer models. As a result, technicians working with such equipment must exercise additional caution and adhere to specific protocols to ensure that the evacuation process minimizes the release of refrigerants into the atmosphere. The primary focus should be on achieving as complete an evacuation as possible, even if the process is more time-consuming and requires more manual oversight. It is imperative to monitor the system closely for any signs of residual refrigerant, as older equipment may not be as effective in detecting and removing all traces of refrigerant from the system. On the other hand, equipment manufactured after November 15, 1993, is subject to more stringent manufacturing and performance standards. These newer models are designed with enhanced capabilities for detecting and recovering refrigerants, thereby reducing the risk of accidental releases during the evacuation process. Technicians using this modern equipment can rely on more automated processes and sophisticated sensors to ensure a thorough evacuation. The focus with these newer systems is not only on efficiency but also on compliance with environmental protection standards, reflecting the industry's shift towards more sustainable practices.

Regardless of the equipment's age, technicians must ensure that they are following all relevant guidelines and regulations. This includes adhering to the Environmental Protection Agency's (EPA) standards for refrigerant recovery and recycling, which are designed to protect the environment and reduce the impact of harmful substances on the ozone layer. Proper training and certification are essential for technicians to stay updated on the latest requirements and best practices in refrigerant recovery and recycling. In addition to regulatory compliance, technicians should also prioritize safety when working with refrigerants. This includes using personal protective equipment (PPE) and being aware of the potential hazards associated with different types of refrigerants. Safety protocols should be rigorously followed to prevent accidents and ensure the well-being of technicians and those around them.

Ultimately, the goal of the evacuation process is to remove refrigerants from low-pressure appliances safely and effectively, regardless of the age of the recovery/recycling equipment. By understanding the specific requirements associated with equipment manufactured before and after November 15, 1993, technicians can adopt the appropriate strategies and techniques to achieve this goal. This not only ensures compliance with environmental regulations but also contributes to the overall sustainability of the HVACR industry.

Pressurizing Low-Pressure Systems

The process of pressurizing low-pressure systems, particularly for non-major repairs, demands a nuanced approach to ensure both the efficacy of the repair and the maintenance of system integrity. Two primary methods have been identified as acceptable for this purpose: the use of controlled hot water and the application of a system heating/pressurization device such as Prevac. Each method has its specific applications, advantages, and considerations that must be thoroughly understood by technicians to apply them effectively.

Utilizing controlled hot water for pressurizing a low-pressure system involves carefully heating water to a predetermined temperature and then circulating this water through the system. This method is particularly useful for its simplicity and the uniformity of the heat distribution it can achieve. The controlled temperature of the water ensures that the system is not subjected to thermal stress that could cause damage. However, technicians must be vigilant in monitoring the temperature and pressure within the system throughout this process to prevent any over-pressurization or overheating, which could compromise the system's integrity. On the other hand, the use of a system heating/pressurization device like Prevac offers a more technologically advanced method for achieving the desired pressurization. These devices are designed to provide a controlled and consistent source of heat that can be precisely regulated to match the requirements of the system being repaired. The advantage of using such a device lies in its ability to rapidly achieve the necessary pressurization levels without the risk of introducing moisture or contaminants into the system, which can be a concern with the controlled hot water method. Additionally, the Prevac system allows for a more hands-off approach to pressurization, enabling technicians to focus on other aspects of the repair process while the system reaches the required pressure.

Regardless of the method chosen, it is imperative that technicians adhere to the manufacturer's guidelines and industry best practices when pressurizing low-pressure systems. This includes ensuring that all safety protocols are followed to protect both the technician and the system from harm. Proper training and certification in the use of these pressurization methods are crucial, as is a thorough understanding of the specific characteristics of the low-pressure system being repaired. By carefully selecting and applying the appropriate pressurization method, technicians can effectively prepare a low-pressure system for non-major repairs, ensuring the longevity and efficiency of the system while upholding the highest standards of safety and environmental responsibility.

Recovery Vacuum Pressure Check

The necessity of waiting a few minutes after achieving the required recovery vacuum to observe if system pressure rises is a critical step in the process of refrigerant recovery from Type 3 Low-Pressure Systems. This practice is not merely a procedural formality but a fundamental aspect of ensuring the thoroughness of the recovery process. The presence of a pressure increase after the system has ostensibly reached the desired vacuum level is indicative of residual refrigerant, either in liquid form within the system or absorbed in the oil. This phenomenon underscores the dynamic nature of refrigerant behavior under vacuum conditions and the capacity of refrigerants to remain concealed within the system components or the compressor oil. The implications of overlooking this step are multifaceted. Firstly, failing to identify and recover all refrigerant could lead to non-compliance with environmental regulations, specifically those aimed at minimizing the release of ozone-depleting substances and greenhouse gases. Secondly, the presence of residual refrigerant can compromise the integrity of subsequent repair or maintenance work, potentially leading to system contamination, inefficiency, or failure. Therefore, the practice of waiting and observing for a pressure rise serves not only as a compliance measure but also as a safeguard against the operational risks associated with incomplete refrigerant recovery.

To implement this step effectively, technicians must be equipped with accurate and sensitive pressure measurement tools capable of detecting even minor fluctuations in system pressure. Digital manifold gauges, which offer precise readings and the ability to monitor changes over time, are particularly suited for this task. Additionally, technicians should be trained to interpret these readings within the context of the specific system being serviced, taking into account factors such as ambient temperature and the physical characteristics of the refrigerant and oil. The process of waiting for a pressure rise also requires a nuanced understanding of the behavior of different refrigerants under vacuum conditions. For instance, refrigerants with a higher boiling point may exhibit a delayed pressure increase as they slowly vaporize from the oil. This characteristic underscores the importance of not only waiting for a few minutes but also knowing how long to wait based on the refrigerant type, system specifications, and environmental conditions. In practice, the procedure involves achieving the target vacuum level, then isolating the system and monitoring the pressure gauge for any increase. If the pressure remains stable, it suggests that the refrigerant has been effectively removed. However, if the pressure begins to rise, further steps must be taken to identify and remove the source of the refrigerant.

This may involve additional recovery cycles, the application of heat to encourage vaporization, or the replacement of contaminated oil. Technicians must document the process meticulously, recording the vacuum level achieved, the duration of the waiting period, any observed pressure increase, and the actions taken in response. This documentation not only serves as a record of compliance with recovery requirements but also provides valuable information for diagnosing and addressing potential issues within the system.

Refrigeration

Purge Unit in Low-Pressure Systems

The purge unit in low-pressure systems plays a critical role in maintaining the efficiency and longevity of refrigeration equipment. Specifically designed for low-pressure chillers, these units are tasked with removing non-condensable gases from the refrigeration cycle. Non-condensable gases, such as air, can enter the system through leaks or during maintenance activities. Their presence in the refrigeration cycle can significantly reduce system efficiency by increasing the head pressure in the condenser. This inefficiency leads to higher energy consumption and, consequently, increased operational costs. Furthermore, the accumulation of non-condensable gases can cause excessive wear on system components, potentially leading to premature failure and the need for costly repairs or replacements. The operation of a purge unit is relatively straightforward yet highly effective. It works by creating a low-pressure area within the unit, which draws the non-condensable gases out of the refrigeration system. These gases are then vented safely out of the purge unit, while the refrigerant, due to its higher boiling point compared to the non-condensables, remains within the system. This process not only improves the thermal efficiency of the chiller but also contributes to the overall reliability of the system by preventing the detrimental effects that non-condensable gases can have on refrigeration components. Regular monitoring and maintenance of the purge unit are essential to ensure its effective operation. Technicians should routinely check the purge unit for signs of wear or malfunction and ensure that it is operating within the manufacturer's specifications. Properly functioning purge units are a key component in the operation of low-pressure refrigeration systems, helping to maintain optimal performance and prevent unnecessary energy usage.

Pressure-Temperature in Low-Pressure Refrigerants

Understanding the pressure-temperature relationships of low-pressure refrigerants is crucial for HVACR technicians working with Type 3 Low-Pressure Systems. These relationships are fundamental to diagnosing, servicing, and maintaining refrigeration equipment efficiently and effectively. Low-pressure refrigerants, such as R-123 and R-11, exhibit specific behaviors under varying temperatures and pressures that are essential to grasp for anyone involved in the HVACR industry. The pressure-temperature (P-T) relationship is a direct correlation between the physical pressure of the refrigerant and its temperature. For low-pressure refrigerants, this relationship is particularly important during the phases of charging, recovery, and troubleshooting of refrigeration systems.

The P-T relationship helps technicians determine the correct refrigerant charge and diagnose system issues. For example, if the pressure of the refrigerant is lower than what the P-T chart specifies for a given temperature, this could indicate a system undercharge or a potential leak. Conversely, higher pressures might suggest an overcharge or restrictions in the system. This diagnostic tool is invaluable for ensuring systems operate at peak efficiency, minimizing environmental impact, and reducing operational costs. In the context of environmental responsibility, understanding the P-T relationship also aids in identifying the phase of the refrigerant (liquid or vapor) at any given point in the system. This knowledge is critical when recovering refrigerant, as it ensures that the recovery process is conducted safely and in compliance with EPA regulations, preventing the release of refrigerants into the atmosphere.

Technicians must be familiar with using P-T charts, which provide the necessary data to interpret the pressure and temperature readings accurately. These charts are specific to each refrigerant type and are an essential tool in the HVACR technician's toolkit. The ability to read and understand these charts is not only a skill that enhances a technician's capability to perform their job but also contributes to their professional growth and the advancement of their career. Moreover, the application of the P-T relationship extends beyond diagnostics and charging. It plays a significant role in the design and selection of HVACR equipment, ensuring compatibility with the specific refrigerants and operational requirements of each system. This aspect underscores the importance of a comprehensive understanding of refrigerants and their behaviors, aligning with the ambitions and career-focused nature of the book's intended audience. For those new to the field or with varying levels of knowledge on the topic, grasping the fundamentals of the P-T relationship is a stepping stone to mastering more complex concepts in refrigeration and air conditioning systems. It provides a solid foundation upon which to build a deeper understanding of refrigeration cycles, system components, and the environmental impacts of refrigerant handling. The practical implications of this knowledge are vast, impacting not only the efficiency and effectiveness of HVACR systems but also contributing to environmental sustainability efforts. By ensuring that refrigerants are handled correctly, recovered fully, and charged accurately according to the P-T relationship, technicians play a direct role in reducing the HVACR industry's environmental footprint. This responsibility aligns with the environmentally conscious values of the audience, emphasizing the importance of professional growth that incorporates a strong understanding of environmental stewardship.

In the fast-paced, work-centric lifestyle of the modern HVACR technician, having a clear and concise resource that elucidates the pressure-temperature relationships of low-pressure refrigerants is invaluable. It enables quick, on-the-job reference and supports the ongoing pursuit of knowledge, efficiency, and environmental responsibility. This section, therefore, not only aims to educate but also to empower technicians with the information necessary to make informed decisions, enhance their skill set, and progress in their careers while upholding the highest standards of environmental and professional integrity.

Safety

ASHRAE 15 Equipment Room Requirements

Adhering to ASHRAE Standard 15, it is imperative for equipment rooms housing refrigeration systems, especially those pertaining to Type 3 Low-Pressure Systems, to be equipped with oxygen deprivation sensors. This requirement underscores the critical importance of maintaining a safe working environment, given the potential hazards associated with refrigerant leaks. Refrigerants, by their nature, can displace oxygen, creating an environment where oxygen levels may fall below safe breathing levels, posing serious risks of asphyxiation to personnel within the vicinity.

The installation of oxygen deprivation sensors serves as a proactive measure to detect and alert personnel to dangerous reductions in oxygen levels, allowing for timely evacuation and intervention measures to be implemented. These sensors are designed to provide real-time monitoring of the air quality within equipment rooms and trigger alarms when oxygen levels drop to a threshold that is considered unsafe for human exposure. The specific threshold at which these alarms are set is determined based on the guidelines provided by ASHRAE Standard 15, which takes into account the volume of the room, the types of refrigerants used, and the maximum quantity of refrigerant that could potentially be released into the atmosphere within the equipment room. In addition to the installation of oxygen deprivation sensors, ASHRAE Standard 15 also mandates the implementation of adequate ventilation systems. These systems are essential for ensuring that any refrigerant leaks are quickly diluted with fresh air, further mitigating the risk of oxygen displacement and ensuring that the concentration of refrigerants in the air remains below flammability or toxicity thresholds. The combination of oxygen deprivation sensors and effective ventilation systems forms a comprehensive safety protocol that significantly enhances the safety of equipment rooms, protecting both the personnel and the integrity of the refrigeration systems housed within. It is crucial for facility managers and

HVACR professionals to adhere to these requirements, not only to comply with regulatory standards but also to uphold the highest standards of safety and health in operational environments. Regular maintenance and testing of both the oxygen deprivation sensors and ventilation systems are also essential to ensure their continued effectiveness in safeguarding against the risks associated with refrigerant leaks.

ASHRAE 15: R-123 Refrigerant Sensor

Focusing on the specific requirements for R-123 refrigerant sensors as mandated by ASHRAE Standard 15, it's crucial to understand the significance of these sensors in maintaining a safe environment within equipment rooms. R-123, being a low-pressure refrigerant, is commonly used in large-scale air-conditioning systems, including centrifugal chillers, which are prevalent in commercial and industrial settings. The nature of R-123 as a chlorofluorocarbon (CFC) necessitates stringent monitoring due to its potential environmental impact and the health risks posed by its leakage.

ASHRAE Standard 15 stipulates that equipment rooms containing systems that use R-123 must be equipped with refrigerant sensors capable of detecting the presence of this specific chemical compound. These sensors are critical for early detection of leaks, allowing for immediate corrective actions to be taken to prevent the accumulation of refrigerant in areas that could endanger human health or contribute to environmental degradation. The requirement for a refrigerant sensor for R-123 underscores the importance of targeted monitoring, given the unique properties and potential risks associated with this refrigerant. The implementation of refrigerant sensors for R-123 also aligns with broader safety and environmental protection goals. By ensuring that any release of R-123 is quickly identified and addressed, facility managers can significantly reduce the risk of exposure to harmful concentrations of this refrigerant. Moreover, this proactive approach to leak detection and management is in line with the principles of responsible refrigerant use, emphasizing the need to minimize leaks and their associated impacts. In practice, the installation of R-123 refrigerant sensors involves selecting devices that are specifically calibrated for this refrigerant, ensuring accurate detection and measurement. These sensors should be strategically placed in locations where leaks are most likely to occur or where refrigerant would accumulate, such as near the floor of the equipment room, given R-123's higher density compared to air. Regular maintenance and calibration of these sensors are also essential to maintain their accuracy and reliability over time, ensuring they continue to provide effective monitoring and contribute to the overall safety of the facility.

Conclusion

Embarking on the journey to achieve EPA 608 certification is a significant step towards not only enhancing one's professional credentials but also contributing to environmental protection efforts. The comprehensive coverage of topics such as the environmental impacts of refrigerants, the Clean Air Act and Montreal Protocol, and the specifics of refrigeration and recovery techniques, underscores the critical nature of this certification in the HVACR industry. It is essential for technicians to possess a deep understanding of these subjects, not only to pass the exam but to apply this knowledge in their daily work, ensuring that they operate in compliance with regulations and best practices aimed at reducing ozone depletion and global warming potential.

The importance of adhering to the EPA 608 regulations cannot be overstated. These regulations are designed to minimize the release of ozone-depleting substances and to ensure the safe handling and disposal of refrigerants. By understanding and implementing the procedures for proper refrigerant recovery, recycling, and reclaiming, technicians play a pivotal role in protecting the environment and public health. Furthermore, the knowledge of substitute refrigerants and oils, along with the awareness of their compatibility and potential environmental impacts, is crucial for making informed decisions in the field.

Safety protocols, including the use of personal protective equipment and adherence to safety standards for equipment rooms, are vital components of the EPA 608 certification topics. These protocols are not just regulatory requirements but are essential practices that safeguard the health and safety of technicians and those around them. The detailed discussion on refrigerant states, pressures, and the refrigeration cycle provides technicians with the foundational knowledge necessary to diagnose and repair HVACR systems efficiently and safely.

As the HVACR industry evolves, with new technologies and refrigerants being introduced, the significance of EPA 608 certification continues to grow. It serves as a testament to a technician's commitment to professionalism, environmental stewardship, and personal growth. The certification opens up avenues for career advancement, higher pay, and job stability, making it a valuable asset for anyone in the field.

The journey towards EPA 608 certification is a challenging yet rewarding endeavor. It requires dedication, study, and a keen understanding of both theoretical concepts and practical applications. As technicians prepare for the exam, it is crucial to focus on the core topics, understand the nuances of each certification type, and stay updated on the latest regulations and industry best practices. This preparation not only aids in passing the exam but also equips technicians with the knowledge and skills needed to excel in their careers and contribute positively to the environment and society.

The role of continuous education and staying abreast of the latest developments in the HVACR industry cannot be understated. As environmental regulations evolve and new refrigerants are introduced to the market, the EPA 608 certification serves not just as a one-time achievement, but as a foundation for ongoing professional development. Technicians are encouraged to participate in further training and education opportunities to enhance their skills and knowledge. This commitment to lifelong learning ensures that HVACR professionals remain at the forefront of the industry, capable of delivering high-quality services while adhering to the highest environmental and safety standards.

Moreover, the EPA 608 certification process emphasizes the importance of ethical practices in the HVACR industry. It instills a sense of responsibility among technicians to perform their duties with integrity, ensuring that refrigerant recovery and recycling are carried out in accordance with legal and environmental guidelines. This ethical approach not only protects the environment but also builds trust with clients, establishing a reputation for reliability and professionalism in the field.

In addition to the technical and ethical aspects covered by the EPA 608 certification, the guide also highlights the importance of effective communication and documentation. Technicians must be adept at communicating complex information in a clear and understandable manner, whether it be explaining the significance of refrigerant recovery to a client or documenting the procedures followed during a service call. These soft skills are essential for ensuring compliance with regulations, facilitating successful audits, and maintaining accurate records for future reference.

The EPA 608 certification guide, therefore, serves as a comprehensive resource for technicians seeking to excel in the HVACR industry. It covers a wide range of topics, from the technical details of refrigerant types and recovery techniques to the broader implications of environmental regulations and the importance of ethical practices. By mastering the content of this guide, technicians not only prepare themselves to pass the EPA 608 exam but also position themselves as knowledgeable and responsible professionals committed to excellence in their field.

As the demand for skilled HVACR technicians continues to grow, the value of EPA 608 certification becomes increasingly apparent. It is a mark of distinction that signifies a technician's dedication to their craft, their commitment to environmental protection, and their readiness to meet the challenges of a rapidly evolving industry. For those aspiring to reach new heights in their HVACR careers, achieving EPA 608 certification is not just a goal but a stepping stone to greater opportunities and success in the field.

Made in the USA
Coppell, TX
09 June 2025

50003322R10063